Roots of Justice

STORIES OF ORGANIZING IN COMMUNITIES OF COLOR

by Larry R. Salomon
Foreword by Elizabeth Martinez

JOSSEY-BASS
A Wiley Imprint
www.josseybass.com

Published by Jossey-Bass
A Wiley Imprint
989 Market Street, San Francisco, CA 94103-1741   www.josseybass.com

Jossey-Bass books and products are available through most bookstores. To contact Jossey-Bass directly call our Customer Care Department within the U.S. at 800-956-7739, outside the U.S. at 317-572-3986 or fax 317-572-4002.

Jossey-Bass also publishes its books in a variety of electronic formats. Some content that appears in print may not be available in electronic books.

Library of Congress Catalog Card Number: 97-77933

ISBN 0-7879-6178-7

Printed in the United States of America
FIRST EDITION
HB Printing   10 9 8 7 6 5 4 3

Chardon Press is grateful to the Applied Research Center of Oakland, California for their financial help in making this book possible. For more information on the Applied Research Center, visit their web site at www.arc.org.

Cover and Book Design by Cici Kinsman, C² Graphics, Oakland, California

Front and back cover images:

Front Cover (top to bottom):

Farmworkers wave the flag of the United Farm Workers at the end of a march in Watsonville, CA in 1996. Photo by David Bacon.

Chinatown activists demonstrate support in 1975 for the I-Hotel. From left to right: William Fong, Olden Ng, unidentified I-Hotel tenant, and Harvey Dong. Photo courtesy of Asian Community Center Archive and Harvey Dong.

Young organizers prepare to lead high school and college students on a march through California in support of affirmative action, 1996. Photo by Scott Braley.

Back Cover:

International Hotel poster. Produced by the San Francisco Poster Brigade, circa 1977. Courtesy of the Asian Community Center Archive and Harvey Dong.

Photo of Larry Salomon by Wallace P. Scott III.

Table of Contents

Foreword

The United States has long been one of the world's most ahistorical societies. Up to middle-age, most people usually feel no connection with events going back more than ten years or so, unless they are personal. The Vietnam War, for example, has little reality for most of today's college students.

Even worse, this is a predominantly anti-historical society, where the past is taught so selectively that it becomes a costumed pageant of heroic stick-figures who come in the same color and gender. Genocide, enslavement and expansion have been institutionally muted to the point of non-existence; the dominant society does not want them seen as the three main building blocks of the original nation. From birth, the United States has emphasized its uniqueness as a country unfettered by tradition, thereby veiling some very ugly and deep-rooted traditions. If history is collective memory, then we must ask: *whose* collective memory?

Such denial means that students may be given information about individual U.S. heroes (and some heroines, today) or isolated events, but not an awareness of ongoing, popular struggle for social justice as basic to this society. Little sense of historical linkage and continuity flows through our public educational system. Nor are youth taught what, or who, really makes history.

We are left in a state of ignorance with serious consequences. Wrong ideas about who makes history, and why, invite a deadly form of disempowerment. To put it bluntly: if you believe history is created primarily by individuals, or by an elite, or by those in power, then why would you think the nameless of our planet could possibly make it a decent place to live?

And that's the first reason why Larry Salomon's book is a treasure-trove. His stories show us that in fact it is the nameless who make the movements that make change. Rather than recounting the lives of individual leaders—which also has value—he offers biographies of struggles and of the communities that waged them. As a result, the issues themselves come to life in new ways. For example, the chapter on the 1963–64 Mississippi Freedom Democratic Party challenge, which I experienced firsthand, illuminates that experience by keeping the people of Mississippi firmly in focus. With another chapter, Salomon effectively puts the Native American occupation of Alcatraz Island in context, showing why it could ultimately be called a victory. His account of the 1943 "Zoot Suit Riots," in which sailors on leave attacked Chicanos wearing a youthful fashion of the time, sees how they helped to spark the 1960s *movimiento* that exploded 25 years later. That sense of linkage and cultural connection is particularly needed for Chicano/a history, too often reduced to a tale of recent immigrants when in fact Mexican people were here before the Pilgrims (albeit as servants of Spanish *conquistadores*).

Those who already know the stories in this collection will learn something new from them again and again, as I did. Those who knew nothing previously are in for eye-opening and inspiring discoveries. The sheer accumulation of struggles for social justice makes a lesson in itself, especially today after almost 20 years of cultivated pessimism and cynicism. For young people who have grown up in today's counter-revolutionary climate beginning in the late 1970s and symbolized by Ronald Reagan, Salomon's book is essential—indeed precious. It is also very vivid, very readable.

The author says in his introduction that he chose the stories told here because they highlight people's ability to control their own destiny. In other words, they can motivate us. Equally important is his belief that the stories show "The work that goes on today had a mama and a papa." Those words summarize a different worldview from that of the dominant society. They speak to human effort as continuous, with a long-range sense of time that reaches beyond our usual western, capitalist definition of "here today, gone tomorrow." This book says: we have news for you, boss. People in struggle have been around a long time, and they're not going away tomorrow.

—Elizabeth (Betita) Martinez

Author's Note

A few years back the editorial board of *Third Force* magazine, of which I was a member, talked about having a regular department to feature past movements in communities of color. Since the magazine was devoted to reporting on and analyzing the latest organizing efforts in these communities, the idea of "looking backward" to remind us of how we got to where we are seemed appealing. The domain of the "Movement History" column soon belonged to me. But I wouldn't be honest if I didn't pay special tribute to a few people.

First, I thank *Third Force* managing editor and publisher John Anner for all his support, help and inspiration. John recruited me to the editorial board of the magazine. He was a great editor, offering constant suggestions and insight. He also got the ball rolling on this book project and provided a lot of editing support. Without him, these pages would not be here. (John has since become executive director of Independent Press Associaiton.)

I also want to acknowledge a fellow *Third Force* board member, Andrea Lewis, for continuing to bother me about the idea of putting the growing stack of "Movement History" columns into book form. Andrea has been a constant source of inspiration, a fellow "Sports-Center" aficionado and a great friend.

Thank you also to the Center for Third World Organizing for giving me the support I needed to work on this project. There would be a chapter in here on CTWO's work over the years, but frankly I would need more time and plenty more pages. I also would like to thank the folks at Chardon Press for believing this book was important enough to publish. Thanks also to Nancy Adess for her incredible editing, which made my writing sound as intelligible as possible.

To my family, who I wished lived closer to me, to Abuelito's memory and to Rona—I dedicate this book. And to all those people whose work is recounted in the following chapters and to those today who do the work and still get left out of the story, you are the ones who make the writing worth doing at all.

—Oakland, CA, November 1997

Introduction

All those histories of this country centered on the Founding Fathers and the Presidents weigh oppressively on the capacity of the ordinary citizen to act. They suggest that in times of crisis we must look to someone to save us: in the Revolutionary crisis, the Founding Fathers; in the slavery crisis, Lincoln; in the Depression, Roosevelt; in the Vietnam-Watergate crisis, Carter. And that between occasional crises everything is all right, and it is sufficient for us to be restored to that normal state. They teach us that the supreme act of citizenship is to choose among saviors, by going into a voting booth every four years to choose between two white and well-off Anglo-Saxon males of inoffensive personality and orthodox opinions.

The idea of saviors has been built into the entire culture, beyond politics. We have learned to look to stars, leaders, experts in every field, thus surrendering our own strength, demeaning our own ability, obliterating our own selves. But from time to time, Americans reject that idea and rebel.

—Howard Zinn, *A People's History of the United States*[1]

This book tells the stories of some of those rebellions. They have been chosen because they highlight our ability to control our destinies. The people written about in this book are not the ones we are accustomed to hearing from or about. They are not the politicians, celebrities, or experts who garner so much popular attention. But because of the work of the people described in this book, because of their legacy of fighting back, we have come to where we are today and we understand better how to keep fighting for the justice that must come if the society we live in is to be truly free.

The stories in this book shy away from the "usual suspects" in social movement histories. They do not glorify the messiahs and big personalities. These leaders played their roles, to be sure, but in focusing on them, movement history makes the same mistake that Zinn warns against: glorifying heroes at the expense of relating the efforts of regular people who, pushed around for years, decided to organize and fight. Those are the people who are the heroes in this book.

Movements for social justice have never arisen because some great leader decided to take charge and lead his (usually) people to the promised land. This mythology makes for predictable Hollywood screen material, but real life never happens that way. The same is true of the spontaneity theory, that is, that movements come "out of nowhere"—without planning, organizing, or long-term programs. They simply explode onto the scene.

Both of these fictions often promulgated in historical writing tend to reduce the vital role played by community organizers. For example, the movement to desegregate the buses in Montgomery didn't happen just because Martin Luther King arrived on the scene or even because Rosa Parks got herself arrested. In fact, there was a whole network in place, including organizations like the Women's Political Council and community people like E.D. Nixon, who had been looking for the right moment to hit back against white supremacy. Without them, there would not have been a Montgomery bus boycott and the civil rights movement would have to trace its beginnings elsewhere.

Affirmative action didn't come into existence because Lyndon Johnson woke up in an enlightened state one day and decided to create Executive Order 11246, which put affirmative action into legal existence. He, and the Congress and the governors and the mayors and the corporations grudgingly accepted demands for affirmative action because they came from the streets and could no longer be ignored. The history of the San Francisco civil rights movement and its demands for employment predate Johnson's consciousness. That story follows on these pages.

So why write about these events today? What's so important about some outdated movements from a forgotten past? Our challenges stare us in the face today. History is for the library. Or the birds.

But it is precisely because those movements can inspire and

motivate our current work that we need to take time to think about what came before us. The work that goes on today had a mama and a papa. Organizers and activists need not feel isolated if they can see the tradition they are continuing with their sweat. And these stories can lift us up, especially when we consider that, almost without exception, they took place against incredible odds.

These stories shed light on some interesting eras, personalities, and creative strategies; they expose painful moments, difficult times and tremendous, seemingly insurmountable obstacles. We need to remember that it is because people moved together and demanded justice in the asparagus fields or the right to vote or some extra money to buy their kids clothes in the wintertime or that attention be paid to any number of injustices suffered by poor people and people of color that we have come as far as we have.

The following pages look back at some interesting movements, some well known, some hardly remembered at all.

The chapter on the welfare rights movement, for example, recalls that in the 1960s and 1970s, poor folks were able to build a movement to demand that a rich society provide some basic services and benefits.

The chapter on the jobs movement in San Francisco during the early 1960s provides a fresh perspective on the history of affirmative action. The struggle for community control of the schools in New York City demonstrates that the need for quality education has been a continuing battle and offers a glimpse into the possibilities of two different communities—African American and Puerto Rican— working together to see that their children share in the same dream.

Not all of the chapters deal with victories. When a friend heard I was including the struggle to save San Francisco's International Hotel, he remarked, "Didn't we lose that one?" The Trail of Broken Treaties, likewise, was a dismal failure if viewed from the perspective of the national media spotlight, which only recorded the vandalism of a federal building. But both the movement to defend elderly Asian tenants and the cross-country caravan of Native Americans raised important issues and inspired lasting work.

The Zoot Suit Riots, on the surface, have little to do with community organizing. But what came from those terrible days in 1943 was also of enduring significance: A whole generation of Chicano activists traced their politicization and commitment to seeing that their communities would be victims no more to those events.

Though the Underground Railroad to help slaves escape to freedom dissolved well over a century ago, retelling the story of its organizing draws us back to a time when a "freedom movement" was literally so.

Other campaigns are remembered here, too. The struggle to free Mississippi from the grips of white supremacy is told from the perspective of those who dedicated their lives to freedom by doing the "slow and respectful" work of day-to-day organizing. The occupation of Alcatraz and the flurry of Indian activism it engendered is told right next to the methods used by Sansei (third-generation Japanese American) activists to win redress and reparations for the imprisonment of their parents and grandparents in the U.S. during World War II.

Some lesser known stories are covered here, too. The efforts of Filipino farm laborers to unionize under the most brutal and violent work and social conditions in California get a stage next to an almost forgotten chapter in Chicano history in which Mexican American women picked up the fight against a paternalistic and unfair mining company in New Mexico during the placid 1950s.

None of these chapters, with the exception of the piece on the San Francisco jobs movement, comes from original scholarship. I borrow heavily on other published sources, looking only to give a condensed, but basically complete version of what happened. Still this book owes a great debt to all of those who first pieced together the histories from which these stories are based. Citations to the many authors and producers of the original material can be found in the references. The chapter end notes refer only to direct quotations. These stories are not intended for academic specialists, but it is my hope that those with the benefits of resources and research money will see in the following pages material inspirational enough to follow up on.

Though the full flavor of each campaign and struggle is necessarily limited in a survey of this type, it is my hope that each chapter will serve as an introduction or a reminder and pique the reader's interest to dig deeper. But even without further research, these stories provide motivation to continue to act for justice and contain important lessons that are relevant for our difficult times.

James Farmer, the former director of the Congress of Racial Equality, talked about the importance of studying history at a conference that joined together the works of scholars and movement people:

> I think that knowledge of the past is vital but historical knowledge is not an end to itself. The more we learn about the past, the more we must recognize that we learn about it in order to bring a more humane society in to being in this country. Otherwise, historical knowledge is meaningless.[2]

One of the better scholars at making historical knowledge meaningful is Charles Payne, author of *I've Got the Light of Freedom*, an excellent book on the organizing tradition and the movement for human dignity in civil rights-era Mississippi. Payne reminds us why history should be retold:

> None of us understands fully how to use what we know of the past to shape a more just present, but we can make sure that social analysis which does not somehow make it clear that ordinary, flawed, everyday sorts of human beings frequently manage to make extraordinary contributions to social change, social analysis which does not make it easier for people to see in themselves and in those around them the potential for controlling their own lives takes us in the wrong direction.[3]

"Roots of Justice" looks at different eras, different communities and their seemingly different needs. But they all shared one thing in common: all were looking for justice and knew that the only way to get it was to fight. The people presented here refused to sit idly by and let others determine their destiny. They fought back. At the risk of sounding romantic, I believe that's the greatest lesson of all, one we would do well never to forget.

NOTES

1. Zinn, *A People's History of the United States*, p. 570.
2. Payne, *I've Got the Light of Freedom*, p. 440.
3. Ibid.

CHAPTER ONE
"I Never Run Off the Track"
Organizing the Underground Railroad

Nathaniel Leach, current historian of Detroit's Second Baptist Church, shows the routes of the Underground Railroad.   Photo by Paul Gainor

Slavery in the United States was a vile institution marked by continuous resistance on the part of the enslaved. While some uprisings and revolts are remembered for their daring and violence, the operation of a clandestine network of "freedom routes" called the Underground Railroad did the most to destroy slavery.

The "conductors" of the Underground Railroad counted on support from abolitionists both Black and white, as well as from many Native American tribes who harbored fugitive slaves. Other activism during the peak years of the abolition movement sought mainly to publicize the inhumanity of slavery. By contrast, the Underground Railroad took the most dangerous direct action short of open revolt by helping slaves actually run away and then helping them again once they did. By the time of the Emancipation Proclamation in 1863, the Underground Railroad posed a serious threat to the slave system.

Southern states had relied on slave labor to grow cotton since colonial days, when about a thousand tons of cotton were being produced annually. But the invention of the cotton gin in 1793 revolutionized southern agriculture, and any hopes of ending slavery based on "moral suasion" were dashed as southern elites became the principal supplier of raw cotton to northern U.S. and European textile industries. (Textiles were the first big commodity of the Industrial Revolution.) By 1860 more than a million tons of cotton were being produced, and the slave population rose from 500,000 to four million Blacks, or one out of every eight Americans.

As the number of slaves increased, so did the mechanisms of repression aimed at keeping them from rebelling. But no matter how harsh the punishment, resistance was constant, including pretending to be sick, destroying property, stealing, engaging in self-mutilation and running away. Federal fugitive slave laws were passed as early as 1793 to return "chattel back to its rightful owner." In fact, laws were passed forbidding slaves to learn to read, play the drums (a signal in many cases that there were people nearby to assist them in escape), become ministers and, of course, travel freely.

Slave catchers threatened both runaways and free Blacks living in the North, who numbered 130,000 in 1830 and nearly 200,000 in 1850. These free Blacks, many of them ex-slaves who had escaped North, were the mainstay of the abolition movement. This community fought passionately for the freedom of their four million brothers and sisters trapped in slavery. It was years before liberal whites and white newspapers would take up the struggle.

In his book *Black Abolitionists*, Benjamin Quarles shows how free Blacks had been organizing around an antislavery, antiracist agenda a full generation before white abolitionists became prominent. Free Blacks worked on a wide range of activities, from organizing all-Black anti-slavery groups, called "vigilance committees," to writing, speaking, petitioning and so on. Frederick Douglass, the famous escaped-slave-turned-abolitionist orator, put it straight to white abolitionists who expected their "Black brethren" to take a back seat when he said in 1853, "It is emphatically our battle; no one else can fight it for us. Instead of depending on [the movement], we must lead it."[1]

No Happy Slaves Here

Several slave revolts during the 19th century were notable for the number of slaves they involved and the extent of their action before being suppressed. These include a rebellion of some thousand slaves led by Gabriel Prosser in an assault on Richmond, Virginia in 1800; an 1811 revolt outside New Orleans where 500 slaves armed with cane knives, axes and other weapons marched from one plantation to the next, killing up to 64 whites, including several slave holders and their families; an uprising in Charleston in 1822 led by Denmark Vesey; and Nat Turner's rebellion in 1831. Turner's uprising had the greatest effect. He and a band of about 70 followers set out to destroy slavery with open warfare. After they killed 57 whites around Southampton, Virginia, a previously nervous white South grew terrified.

Though the value of outright rebellion, with its often suicidal consequences, was hotly debated in the African American community, the single biggest threat to the plantation system became the Underground Railroad.

Running away could cripple the plantation system through the loss of its workforce and was a much more realistic path to freedom than armed revolt. As more and more slaves disappeared, escape from bondage was seen as threatening the established order of the South. During the 1850s, about a thousand slaves ran away every year to the North, into Canada and Mexico and to the refuge of some Native American lands, including the Florida Seminoles. Before the Underground Railroad set up its tracks, the road north was terribly lonely, allies were scarce and pursuit was certain. But in the decades leading up to the Civil War, runaways were helped along by an organized system.

The term "Underground Railroad" is said to have its roots in a legend about an escaped slave named Tice Davids, who ran from his Kentucky owner in the same year as the Turner-led revolt. Davids took refuge in the home of John Rankins, a white abolitionist in Ripley, Ohio. The slave owner and his posse followed Davids to the Ohio River but then completely lost track of him, leaving the confused group wondering if the slave had "gone off on some underground road."[2]

Riding the Underground

The Underground Railroad was about organizing for justice at a time when doing so could cost you your life. By the time the Civil War began in 1861, the URR was a complicated network of vigilance committees, liberty associations, self-defense groups and lookouts. New escape routes were constantly being opened. In the East, for example, "tracks" were laid from Washington, D.C., to Rochester, New York, with stops in New York City, where a militant vigilance committee headed by Black clergyman Charles Ray aided the journeys of "passengers" by providing shelter for a night and directions about where to go next.

Fugitives were hidden by friendly folks everywhere imaginable: livery stables, attics, storerooms, under feather beds and in secret passages. They were disguised in many different masks; they moved from station to station by boat, wagon and train; routes of travel were changed at a moment's notice if danger was anticipated.

The courageous fugitive slaves who took advantage of the URR did so only after completing the most dangerous part of their escape alone and without help, often hiding in swamps and deep woods, following the "drinking gourd" (the Big Dipper constellation that includes the North Star) for guidance. Runaways would look to see on which side of a tree's trunk moss was growing, and head in the direction of the heaviest growth, usually the north side.

There were two primary routes, one from Kentucky to Ohio, the other along the eastern seaboard to Canada. Through Pennsylvania, east, west and north, lines stretched through Philadelphia, Harrisburg, Pittsburgh, or east to Trenton and on through New York and upstate. Tracks ran through Ohio along just about every little town along the Ohio River. Illinois lines snaked though little towns, draining into Chicago or into the capital at Springfield. Iowa and Nebraska had intricate systems, with vigilance committees aiding runaways to safe havens in Milwaukee and Canadian cities.

Slaves who lived in the Deep South would often go to Mexico, the Caribbean or into Native American societies instead of making the dangerous trek north. Many more risked their lives in unpeopled territory crawling with alligators and other scary creatures. The fact that many slaves chose the swamp over the "benevolent" institution of slavery is a good indication of how strong the urge for freedom was.

The federal government gave in to the South's loud complaints about the huge increase in runaways by passing the Fugitive Slave Act of 1850, a legislative package that provided concessions to the slaveocracy by allowing New Mexico, Utah and Texas to be admitted to the Union without restrictions on slavery in return for the admission of California as a non-slave state. The act also made federal assistance available to slave owners trying to reclaim their "chattel" or even capture free Blacks from the North and claim they were slaves. In the infamous Dred Scott case of 1857, the Supreme Court strengthened slave owners' hands when it declared that Negroes "are so inferior that they have no rights which a white man [was] bound to respect."[3]

Organizing in the face of these two developments became even more dangerous. But if federal mandates were supposed to quiet the activity on the underground, they failed. Freedom tracks blossomed all over. If the laws were not going to protect them, Blacks, free and slave, were going to have to organize with even greater determination to protect themselves.

In Syracuse, N.Y., right after President Millard Fillmore signed the Fugitive Slave Act into law, a runaway slave named Jerry was captured by bounty hunters and held at the courthouse. Underground Railroad activists in Syracuse had been heavily organized to defy slavecatchers and anyone else who stood in the way of their station operating smoothly. Ex-slave J.W. Loguen directed much of the operations in town; it is estimated that he helped more than 1,500 runaways reach Canada. As Jerry awaited transport back to the South, word quickly got out to the organized community. Soon a large crowd descended upon the courthouse and with activist Jo Norton and a group of African Americans armed with crowbars and a battering ram, they stormed in to free Jerry. The freed former slave was taken into hiding, given clothes provided by the vigilance committee and whisked away further north, where he lived the rest of his days in freedom. In Syracuse, they celebrated "Jerry Anniversaries" every year until the Civil War.

All Aboard

Those on the "safe" end of the railroad spent a lot of time in enemy territory. The most famous of all "conductors" was a woman the slaves called Moses—Harriet Tubman. In 1849 Tubman escaped from a slave plantation in Maryland. She returned to the South 19 times to help bring more than 300 people (including her elderly parents) to freedom. The historian Henrietta Buckmaster wrote that Tubman "had the strength to lift a man in her arms and run with him if he did not move quickly enough to hide himself from danger, she had the sharp intelligence that met every emergency, and she had the ruthless courage, too, that enabled her to carry a pistol wherever she went and threaten to use it if any of her friends showed timidity." Tubman, who lived much of her days with a $40,000 price on her head, was known to say "I can't die but once." After emancipation, Tubman proudly claimed, "I never run my train off the track and I never lost a passenger."[4]

There were countless other Black women organized in the Underground Railroad and in the larger abolitionist movement. Female vigilance committees functioned as auxiliaries to the larger groups headed by men, but individual women like Josephine St. Pierre Ruffin in Boston and Hetty Reckless in Philadelphia provided much of the leadership without fanfare. Reckless was a key figure in one of the railroad's stops in Philadelphia, helping to provide a support network that provided food, clothing and shelter for runaways. Much of this work was supported entirely by the Black community, since white antislavery societies favored speechmaking over committing funds for Underground Railroad activities. Moral "suasionists" (liberals) and speechmakers were necessary, but many of the Black freedom fighters had themselves escaped slavery and felt more than anything the immediacy of helping their people get freedom. Though they usually worked together, and Blacks relied on the great support of many dedicated and courageous whites, strategic differences still existed and many Blacks formed independent vigilance groups.

One such group, the New York Vigilance Committee, was founded by David Ruggles, a former slave. The New York Vigilance Committee helped more than a thousand fugitives—including Frederick

Douglass, in 1838—escape. Ruggles dedicated his entire life to the cause, incurring the vengeance of white slave supporters more than a few times. Ruggles' New York bookstore was burned down, his house was set on fire, he was jailed several times and he was almost kidnapped by slave catchers on different occasions.

Despite the dangers, historian Vincent Harding tells us, Ruggles continued his work. Not only did his Vigilance Committee provide food, lodging and a support group for Blacks who made it to New York, but "when slave agents apprehended them, Ruggles trailed them from magistrate to magistrate, refusing to leave the Black captives at the mercies of a racist law. Also, taking another tack, he knocked without hesitation on the doors of many white families, demanding information on Black servants suspected of being held there against their will."[5]

Some slaves, like Henry "Box" Brown, devised escape strategies that sound like stories from Hollywood movies. Through contacts in the North, Brown decided that the only way to escape his Virginia owner was to mail himself in a cloth-lined box that was two feet, eight inches deep, two feet wide and three feet long. He had himself packed into the box with only a container of water and a few small biscuits. Despite the "This Side Up" stamp on the box, Brown was handled roughly for days. Finally the shipment reached its destination, the home of several abolitionists in Philadelphia. They opened up the box expecting the worst. Brown emerged and said simply, "How do you do, gentlemen?"[6]

In Chicago, Black antislavery activists organized the Liberty Association, patrolling city streets to look for slavecatchers and assist runways to safe areas. Militant groups of African Americans in Cincinnati, Cleveland, and Oberlin, Ohio, where whites were probably the most widely organized and helpful, formed paramilitary patrols.

On occasion, antislavery activists confronted the slave owners directly. In the town of Christiana, Pennsylvania, in September, 1851, a former slave-turned-freedom fighter named William Parker was ready when Maryland slave owner Edward Gorsuch arrived in pursuit of four escaped slaves. Accompanied by his son, some neighbors and a deputy U.S. marshal, Gorsuch found out where the slaves were being protected.

But by the time Gorsuch arrived at the house where the slaves were hiding to demand his property, the house had been turned into an armed fortress, defended by Parker and his troop of both Blacks and whites. When the slavers threatened to set fire to the house, Parker's wife sounded a horn from the second-story window, calling dozens of supporters to surround Gorsuch's group. Gorsuch refused to leave but likely wished he had. Armed with guns, knives, stones and corn cutters, the crowd converged on the would-be kidnappers, killing all but the marshal. A contingent of U.S. Marines was sent in, but Parker and his comrades were gone when they arrived and the slaves were never captured. (The greatest account of experiences of organizing for freedom along the Underground Railroad is William Still's collection, *The Underground Railroad, A Record,* published in 1872.)

Despite the historical myth that Blacks were happy to serve and wished that the crazy whites from up North would leave ol' massa to his affairs, during the Civil War years more than half a million slaves ran away—a huge number, as Howard Zinn notes in *A People's History of the United States,* considering the inevitable confusion about where to go and how to live. Many followed the routes set up by the Underground Railroad and made their way to freedom, joining the thousands of their free brothers and sisters who had worked so hard to make it possible.

The myth that Lincoln freed the slaves or that liberal whites played the leading role in ending slavery is just that—a myth. The organized antislavery movement counted on people like Parker, Ruggles and Tubman, in leaders like Charles and Sarah Remond, J.W.C. Pennington, Robert Purvis, Sojourner Truth, William Still and countless others—committed African Americans willing to take awful risks to change the condition of their people.

NOTES

1. Quarles, *Black Abolitionists,* p. 18.
2. Buckmaster (Henkle), *Let My People Go,* p. 59.
3. Franklin, *From Slavery to Freedom,* p. 178.
4. Buckmaster, p. 213–216.
5. Harding, *There Is a River,* p. 123.
6. Blockson, *The Underground Railroad,* pp. 135–138.

CHAPTER TWO

"Ang Laka Ay Nasa Pagkakaisa"

"Strength is in Union":
Filipino Farmworkers Organize in the 1930s

Filipino union members with tons of donated food destined for the families of striking waterfront workers, 1948. Photo courtesy San Francisco State Labor Archive and Research Center

Mention conditions faced by California farm workers and most people think of Cesar Chavez and the efforts of the United Farm Workers Union (UFW) in the 1960s and 1970s. But the UFW was not the first successful farm worker union in U.S. history. And, contrary to the historical emphasis, Mexican American workers were not the first to establish a militant farm labor agenda. Filipino immigrants Philip Vera Cruz and Larry Dulay Itliong were as instrumental in shaping the direction of farm worker organizing in the 1950s as anyone in the formative years of the Agricultural Workers Organizing Committee (AWOC) and the UFW.

These leaders of the 1950s and 1960s owed a great deal to the pioneering efforts of Filipino workers during the 1930s who organized under the banner of the Filipino Labor Union (FLU) at a time when the treatment of agricultural workers—and other people of color—was at its worst.

Filipinos began leaving their homeland shortly after the U.S. took possession of the Philippines at the turn of the 20th century. Pushed by wretched poverty, tens of thousands of the young nationals were lured by the dream of finding prosperity in the Hawaiian sugar cane fields. In the 1920s, large numbers began coming to mainland America, where early work in the California orchards and the Alaskan fisheries was available. The allure of America was especially strong for this new generation of Filipinos that had been raised speaking English in American schools in the Philippines. They had been told wonderful stories about American democracy, freedom and how even the poorest of farmers could one day own a plot of land and make bushels-full of money. Work was there for the taking.

In 1920, there were just over 5,000 Filipinos on the U.S. mainland. By 1930, after immigration laws were passed to cut off the influx of Chinese and Japanese immigrants, the Filipino population grew to more than 40,000. Most of those were men who planned on being away for only a few years, just long enough to find the great riches the propaganda about the mainland had promised.

Typical was the story of Alfonso Yasonia's arrival to the U.S. Upon landing in San Francisco, the 22–year-old Pinoy didn't spend much time in the city.

> I stayed one week in the International Hotel and then I heard there was work in Stockton. So my friend took me to the Ferry Building and told me to take the ferry. "When the ferry lands," he said, "that is Stockton." The next morning the ferry stopped in Stockton, so I pick up my suitcase and walk around town. I

saw a Filipino restaurant so I go in to eat breakfast. I was there about twenty minutes when somebody walk in and hollers, "Who want work?"[1]

One out of every four Filipino workers worked in the service industries as janitors, houseboys and busboys, where subservience was demanded. "I had to crawl on my knees to please them [white employers]," said one worker. "I had to be submissive and eternally patient."[2]

But most Filipinos who came in the early days worked in agriculture. Contractors placed young workers into work gangs and made them available to the large agribusinesses all over the state. There was no such thing as being settled. Seasonal work meant that you went from place to place.

"We traveled," one Filipino said in the early 1930s. "I mean, we moved from camp to camp." The work was not easy either. "I worked about six hours that first day and when my back was hurting I said to myself: 'Why did I come to this country? I was doing easy in the Philippines.'" Another vineyard worker remembered toiling in the oppressive heat. "It was one hundred and thirteen degrees. I used to get two gallons of water to pour on my head. By the time it reached the ground, I was dry."[3]

California's favorable climate and rich soil allowed farmers to grow more than 300 crops, making agribusiness a lucrative industry for the state in the 1920s. In addition, farmers realized early on that by using cheap, unorganized migratory labor—mainly Chinese, Japanese, Mexican and Filipino men—they could keep the cost of production down.

Filipinos comprised nearly the entire asparagus-picking work force in the Sacramento and San Joaquin Valleys and handled more than 80 percent of the Salinas Valley lettuce crop. They were also employed in harvesting rice, fruit, sugar beets and grapes and in celery planting and general ranch labor.

As the newest recruits into the labor force, Filipino workers were paid the lowest wages. In the case of certain crops, like asparagus, these wages were further diminished as growers found it more profitable to work more laborers per acre at a lower wage per worker, ensuring efficient and more productive harvesting.

Many of the larger growers looked upon Filipinos as perfectly suited for the kind of back-breaking labor needed in their fields. Cutting asparagus, planting cauliflower and other "stoop labor" was ideal for Filipinos, wrote white newspaper editors. "White men can't do the work as well as these short men who can get down on their hands and knees, or work all day long stooping over." But the Filipino workers, with all their aches and pains, knew better.

It soon became apparent that the dreams of American opportunity and greatness were not to be found in the fields. The America on celluloid was much different from the one these immigrants found. Legendary farmworker organizer Philip Vera Cruz, wrote about the frustrations of these early immigrants in his famous poem called "Profits Enslave the World":

> But beautiful bright pictures painted
> Were just half of the whole story...
> Reflections of great wealth and power
> In the land of slavery[4]

Typically paternalistic and complacent, the big growers believed that labor organization was too complex for young Filipinos to master. Instead, they believed, these workers were ripe for exploitation and, true to the Asian stereotype, would be docile and uncomplaining. Apparently the growers were ignorant of labor history in Hawaii, where Filipino and Japanese laborers, in a show of interethnic solidarity, went on strike in 1919. In that action, three thousand Filipino workers demanded that sugar planters pay higher wages, provide an eight-hour work day, create an insurance fund for retired employees and give paid maternity leave. Soon five thousand Japanese workers joined them. Despite attempts by the owners to break the strike by importing laborers from other countries, the workers won most of their demands. Eventually the two unions joined together in the Hawaii Laborers Association.[5]

The "Filipino Labor Menace"

When conditions demanded a similar response in California's fields, many Filipino workers brought organizing sophistication and experience from their involvement in work slow-downs, stoppages and full-fledged strikes in Hawaii. In addition, most Filipinos had been imbued with a sense of democratic principles. "That's what they [Americans] kept pushing in their history books when we were growing up," one worker recalled. "We didn't think of ourselves as inferior to whites. We knew we were their equals and we were not about to be pushed around."[6]

Soon enough, the growers knew it too. As early as 1924, some were complaining about how independent and hard to manage the workers from the Philippines were. As the U.S. entered into the Great Depression, farm wages fell through the floor. Many farm workers quickly realized that they had to do something to keep from starving. Unlike other industries, California agribusiness remained profitable during the depression. So when their wages were cut, Filipinos began to walk off the job in protest. Many workers called for union support from the mainstream American Federation of Labor (AFL) unions.

White AFL leaders were startled by the aggressive pro-union stance of Filipino workers, but they made their view clear that the "Filipino labor menace" represented unfair competition to white labor and could not be included in their unions. Rejected by the mainstream labor movement, Filipino organizers built their own unions.

Most of the early attempts at unionization, like the Sons of the Farm, Inc., Filipino Labor Association of Stockton and the Filipino United Labor Economic Endeavor were small in membership and politically ineffective. Nevertheless, they exploded the myth of a docile Asian labor force and set the stage for a larger movement. In fact, once Filipino workers became the dominant work force in a commodity such as lettuce, asparagus, figs and other crops, they began demanding better wages and working conditions. Docile they definitely were not.

The drive to organize got a sharp stick in the ribs from local white civic organizations like the American Legion, who, aided by the police and the media in the 1930s, provoked violent mob riots aimed at Filipinos throughout the state. "In many ways it was a crime to be a Filipino in California," explained Filipino union organizer and writer Carlos Bulosan. For Bulosan, living in "the fascist state of California" forced Filipino workers to develop both race and

Striking Filipino asparagus workers march through the streets of downtown Stockton, 1948.
Photo courtesy San Francisco State Labor Archive and Research Center

class consciousness. Filipino labor leaders believed that the right to demand better wages would lead to a decline in racial tension and social inequality. If Filipinos were allowed to join unions with whites, they felt, a spirit of brotherhood would prevail.[7]

Meanwhile, violence against Filipinos was on the rise. In 1926, police joined groups like the Native Sons of the Golden West and the American Legion in harassing workers into leaving the San Joaquin Valley. After a farm worker organizer was killed in El Centro, fear also gripped the Imperial Valley further south. Bulosan later wrote about the anxiety many Filipinos felt. "I wanted to leave, but José (a friend and fellow worker) insisted that we work through the season. I worked but made myself inconspicuous. At night, I slept with a long knife under my pillow. My ears became sensitive to sounds and even my sense of smell was sharpened. I knew when rabbits were mating between the rows of peas. I knew when night birds were feasting in the melon patches."[8]

Generalized anti-Filipino racism was growing. In the media, Filipinos were stereotyped as "criminally prone and troublemakers." They were described as "jungle savages" from a primitive culture. Worst of all, these slanders were coming from educators, politicians and business leaders, all of whom apparently felt they were expert about Filipinos. The former president of the University of California, David T. Barrows, testified in 1929 before a U.S. Congressional committee on immigration that Filipinos brought tremendous problems to the states with them. They were, according to Barrows, aroused by an inordinate level of sexual passion and had a natural tendency for vice and crime.[9]

Some white workers resorted to violence and mob attack. In Washington's Yakima Valley in 1928, two carloads of sixty Fillipinos heading for work on apple farms were run out of town by a mob of about 150 whites, who threatened to shoot them. Others tried to intimidate Filipinos as well as those who would put them to work. One grower in California was told, "Work no Filipinos or we'll destroy your crop and you too." Another threat went to the police: "Get rid of all Filipinos or we'll burn this town down." Several Filipino workers were beaten by mobs, some were even killed.[10]

In Watsonville, the worst of what was called a "race-riot" exploded in late 1929 and early the next year. After the local newspaper printed pictures of a young Filipino man embracing his white fiancée, a frenzy of racism spread through the town. Daily headlines such as, "The Filipino Is The State's Next Problem" and "State Organizations Will Fight Filipino Influx Into County," contributed to the tense atmosphere. Filipinos soon came under attack in the streets on a regular basis.

Then, on January 19, 1930, white mobs attacked a Filipino dance hall, touching off four consecutive days of violence. At one point, the mob grew to more than 700 white men. Many Filipinos were clubbed by the angry mobs, whose numbers were swelled by police. A young Filipino lettuce picker, Fermin Tabera, was shot and killed.

After that, even the California Athletic Commission banned Filipino boxers from fighting because of the fear of inciting hostile white crowds. To top it all off, Filipinos were being blamed for the violence.

Stand Your Ground and Fight

The farm workers knew they had only two choices. They could accommodate the white hatred and flee from the terrorism, or they could stand their ground and become militant. Though scared, they learned from the events in Watsonville and across the state not to give in to the intimidation. In Los Angeles, labor leader Pablo Manlapit organized a march of more than 1,000 sympathizers protesting Tabera's murder. "To the Pinoy laborers," writes Roberto Vallangca, in his book, *Pinoy: The First Wave,* "Fermin Tabera became a martyr."[11]

Fighting back meant organizing for justice on two fronts at the same time, against both exploitation and violent racist attacks.

The struggle for better working conditions was given a decided boost when the Trade Union Unity League founded the Agricultural Workers Industrial League in 1930. The organization was set up to initiate large-scale unionization of Filipino workers and threaten field owners with the possibility of paralyzing strikes. Authorities and the press accused the workers of being Communist dupes because the League was Communist-led. However, despite charges to the contrary, the majority of Filipinos refused to become active members of the Communist Party because, according to many of the farm workers themselves, Communist labor organizers showed little respect for Filipino culture and traditions and seemed especially condescending.

The Filipino Labor Union Strikes Salinas in 1934

Organizing in the California fields intensified in the 1930s, particularly in Salinas, the self-proclaimed "Salad Bowl of the World." The fields were owned by a relatively small group of big capitalist farmers, many of whom lived outside of the region or the state. Wages for farm workers had been cut in half between 1930–1933 while profits for the growers increased, thanks largely to government subsidies. As more Filipino workers migrated to Salinas to work the lettuce fields and met deplorable working conditions and low wages as well as incessant racism, work to unionize moved forward.

According to historian Howard De Witt, the key figure in developing the Filipino Labor Union (FLU) was Pablo Manlapit, who had worked as a laborer and organizer in Hawaii before arriving on the mainland. It was Manlapit who had formed the first FLU, which struck against Hawaiian plantations in 1919 and 1924. Driven out of Hawaii, Manlapit journeyed to Stockton to try to organize a stateside FLU. Though he left before the FLU was formed in California, he should be credited with getting the ball rolling.

In 1933, Rufo Canete, D.L. Marcuelo and other Filipino labor leaders met in Salinas and picked up where Manlapit left off by officially organizing the mainland FLU. Under the leadership of Canete, Marcuelo, Johnny Estigoy, Nick Losada and others, the FLU grew rapidly to seven chapters and more than 4,000 members. "Ang laka ay nasa pagkakaisa" was their motto ("strength is in union").

Many Filipinos saw the need for racial unity, especially when organizing. "To me," said organizer Antonio Gallego Rodrigo, "it did not matter what island [in the Philippines] they came from or what dialect they spoke. They were all Filipinos like me."[12]

Less than a year after being officially organized, the FLU launched a drive in Salinas to organize farm workers of all nationalities around the goals of an increased minimum wage (to 35 cents per hour), an eight-hour day, employment without racial discrimination, recognition of the union as a bargaining agent and the abolition of labor contractors. Workers also wanted an end to what was called the "hold back" system, in which growers would withhold a portion—usually a fourth—of a worker's pay in order to force the Filipino laborers to work through the whole season.

On their side, the growers were represented by the Associated Farmers of California, arguably the largest, most influential lobby in Sacramento. They were funded by the growers, the California Packing Association, the Southern Pacific Railroad, the Industrial Association of San Francisco, the Holly Sugar Corporation, the Spreckels Investment Company and even the Pacific Gas and Electric Company. It hardly seemed like a fair fight.

Soon after the Salinas demands were rejected, the FLU called the first strike. Almost 7,000 men and women employed in the lettuce fields and packing sheds in Salinas walked out, including white workers who were members of the Vegetable Packers Association, a sometime ally of the FLU. But the white workers soon left the strike and agreed to arbitration. Despite this setback, along with constant intimidation from white vigilantes and even pressure from some conservative segments of the Filipino community to call off the strike, the campaign persisted.

White intimidation increased. Signs went up throughout Salinas like the one that announced: "This is a White Man's Country. Get Out of Here if You Don't Like What We Pay." Law enforcement didn't help either. On the contrary, both the Salinas sheriff and the California Highway Patrol encouraged goon squads to harass the striking workers.

Canete, Marcuelo, Luis Agudo and other leaders toured the camps every day to boost the spirits of Filipino strikers. The strikers stood strong. "As long as we felt that we were not getting justice," one worker recalled, "and so long as we were going to be treated like second-class people, like dogs, we had no choice but to stay away from the fields. We had to fight for our dignity, not just for better wages."[13]

The strike went on for months. It had completely shut down the lucrative lettuce industry until growers brought in strikebreakers from Mexico, India and other parts of Asia. But the damage had been done. The big growers and affiliated businesses, like the Ice-Kist Packing Company, began to feel the pinch on their profits. Having lost up to $100,000 daily during the strike, the growers agreed to terms that were, in most cases, better than the union's original demands.

With their strength renewed, the Filipino labor movement began receiving support in the form of solidarity statements from some corners of organized labor. And while some progress was made in material conditions for Filipino workers, constant intimidation of union leaders by white vigilante mobs across the West Coast reinforced the need for unions with an active interest in protecting people of color.

Keeping the Struggle Alive

The efforts of the FLU were short-lived. The idea of an independent ethnic labor organization had served its purpose, but to most of the workers and many of the FLU leadership, it seemed wiser to join forces with Mexican American and other workers and push for official recognition from the American Federation of Labor.

Filipinos remained committed to labor organizing, as evidenced by the growing popularity of Pablo Manlapit's book, *Filipinos Fight for Justice,* published in the 1930s, which detailed the history of plantation organizing in Hawaii. After another successful, but far shorter, strike against Salinas growers in 1936, the AFL and the California Federation of Labor could no longer ignore the power of Filipino labor strength. In February of 1937, the AFL finally granted a charter to the Field Workers Local No. 30326, a combined Mexican and Filipino union. This gave organizing a decided boost because, with the passage of the National Industrial Recovery Act in 1934, growers were required to recognize legitimate unions.

In 1938, representatives from all the Filipino organizations on the Pacific Coast voted to form the Filipino Agricultural Laborers Association (FALA). However, Filipino organizers such as Francisco Varona, Macario Bautista and Lamberto Malinab believed inclusion of all farm workers was critical, and invited Mexican workers and other ethnic groups into their ranks. They later changed the union's name to the Federated Agricultural Laborers Association.

In 1939, FALA won its most significant victory with a successful strike against the asparagus industry. After a one-day stoppage involving thousands of workers, all 258 growers signed an agreement guaranteeing unprecedented worker rights. The success in the asparagus industry prompted other victories in the celery, Brussels sprouts and garlic fields from San Mateo to San Benito counties. By 1940, there were nearly 30,000 FALA members.

In the late 1950s and 1960s, Philip Vera Cruz, Larry Dulay Itliong, Chris Mensalvas, Ernesto Mangaoang and Pete Velasco helped continue the struggle with a new farm labor movement. This time they were able to begin successfully reaching across ethnic lines for the long haul. Itliong was a key organizer and later the vice-president of the Agricultural Workers Organizing Committee (AWOC). AWOC, formed in 1959 by the AFL-CIO, led the first grape strike in Delano, California, in 1965. Much of the organizing leadership in this first great grape strike was done by energetic young Filipinos like Nacasio Campos, Alfredo Vasquez and Felicin Ytom. AWOC was soon able to convince Cesar Chavez and his small National Farm Workers Association to combine his efforts with theirs. Soon enough, almost all of the region's grape workers were on strike. Shortly after, the two unions merged to form what the United Farm Workers, opening a new era of farmworker organizing, one that would not have been possible without the brave work of Filipinos a generation earlier.

NOTES

1. Vallangca, *Pinoy*, p. 75.

2. Takaki, *In the Heart of Filipino America*, p. 32.

3. Ibid, pp. 36–37.

4. Scherlin and Vilanueva, *Philip Vera Cruz*, p. xi.
This is an interesting personal account from Vera Cruz on how the modern farm worker movement got its start, though there is little on the struggles of the 1930s.

5. Takaki, *Strangers From a Different Shore*, pp. 259–260.

6. Vallangca, p. 79.

7. De Witt, *Violence in the Fields*, pp. 5, 13–14.

8. Bulosan, *America is in the Heart*, p. 144.

9. De Witt, *Violence*, p. 10.

10. Takaki, *In the Heart*, p. 50.

11. Vallangca, p. 24.

12. Cordova, *Filipinos*, p. 73.

13. De Witt, "The Filipino Labor Union."

CHAPTER THREE

The "Zoot Suit Riots"

Pachucos vs. the Navy

Nearly half a million Chicanos served in the U.S. armed forces during World War II, and Chicanos from Los Angeles made up large numbers of those who fought and died. But as returning Black and Asian servicemen also found, heroism in the name of American values on the front lines did not change the virulent racism and bigotry back home. Highly decorated Sergeant Macario Garcia is a good example. One of the very few recipients of the nation's most prestigious military award—the Congressional Medal of Honor—Garcia was unceremoniously thrown out of a restaurant in his hometown in California for trying to buy a cup of coffee after getting back from the front lines.

East Los Angeles, home to the largest and best-known Chicano community in the United States, had suffered for years from Anglo hostility. But soldiers returning to East L.A. after the war refused to tolerate racism at home after fighting it abroad, and the community itself had grown more self-confident and unwilling to tolerate abuse. Thus, when attacked by white military personnel who were on off-duty passes, Chicanos in Los Angeles fought back. The resulting disturbances, which reached their peak over a 10-day period in June 1943, became known as the Zoot Suit Riots.

The Zoot Suit Riots sent shock waves through the Mexican community. Following on the heels of the humiliating mass deportations of the 1930s and the notorious "Sleepy Lagoon" criminal trial (described below), the riots were directly tied to an unprecedented rise in ethnic and political consciousness in the Chicano community. After the riots had ended, the Chicano community looked inward, proud that it could fight back and determined to make certain that its members would no longer be passive victims.

Same Old Song—Disaffection's Roots

Mexicans have been faced with white dominance ever since Anglos took control of California and the Southwest in the middle of the nineteenth century. Mexican immigrants—both those who were naturalized and those who later came from Mexico to find work or escape revolution—struggled against a second-class citizenship that was considered natural in the racial pecking-order.

During the twentieth century, millions more Mexicans fled the ravages of war-torn Mexico and went to "el norte"—California, Texas, Arizona and other places where one could find refuge, opportunity and maybe even freedom. Many found work in California's fertile valleys, but unlike the Asian immigrants among them who were not allowed to bring their wives and children to America, whole families of Mexicans came to the U.S.

Predictably, during an economic crisis, racist elements were quick to attack anyone who was "alien." That came to mean anyone who was not white. During the Great Depression, white Americans clamored for the removal of Mexicans on the grounds that they competed with "real Americans" for jobs and resources.

In 1931, Secretary of Labor William N. Doak requested that Congress authorize the deportation of an estimated half-million undocumented Mexican immigrants from the U.S. In Los Angeles, officials circulated leaflets in Mexican communities that warned of the coming deportations. The leaflets threatened all Mexicans, legal or illegal. Within weeks, thousands of Mexicans were detained. Over the next three years, Los Angeles County sent more than 12,000 Mexicans "back where they came from."

By the time World War II began, fewer than three million Mexican Americans were living in the U.S. During the war, however, many different ethnic groups were lured to U.S. cities to work in defense-related industries. Soon, Los Angeles had the highest concentration of Mexicans outside of Mexico City. Mexicans were segregated in one area of the city and African Americans in another. These two groups occupied the oldest, most run-down housing.

Both felt the effects of strict segregation at many recreational and entertainment facilities that kept out "non-whites."

By the start of U.S. involvement in World War II, there were almost 350,000 Mexican Americans in California, with the majority in Los Angeles. Job discrimination forced many to work for below-poverty-level wages, and the white labor movement generally alienated Chicanos or actively barred them from participating.

The war years also brought large numbers of African Americans to Los Angeles to fill industrial jobs, while Japanese Americans were shipped off to internment camps. Whipped up by a sensationalist media, racism was open and vicious. Headlines in the *Los Angeles Times* warning of "The Scoundrel Jap" and the growing "Negro Problem" were typical. Coverage of the Mexican American community was just as bad. In one story, young Mexican Americans were described as "threatening wolf packs."

Apparently under the impression that Los Angeles was given to whites by God, the newspapers and wartime propaganda machine described Mexicans as aliens "invading" California. Stories of crime and other social problems were always given ethnic specificity. In fact, the government of Mexico complained that the use of terms like "Mexican criminal" instead of simply "criminal" was unjust. As a result, the word "Mexican" was soon replaced in media accounts with the terms "pachuco" or "zoot-suiter"—as though all Mexicans were the same.

Pachucos Defy Convention

Some of the young people—or pachucos, as they were called—belonged to *clicas* (gangs) that carried the name of their neighborhoods—El Hoyo, Alpine Street, White Fence. Within these *clicas* a fad began to spread. Gang members and their imitators—Chicanos, Blacks and whites alike—would dress up in wide-shouldered jackets and baggy pants known as "zoot suits." As with the cultural trappings of today's youth, many onlookers in the 1940s were put off by the zoot-suiters' dress, style and insolent attitude, which explicitly defied the conventional society that excluded them. To the pachucos, mostly low-income youth who spoke a mixture of Spanish, English and words adapted by border Mexicans, the zoot suit was a sign of rebellion, but it was also just fashionable.

A popular hang-out among some of the gangs was a gravel pit used as a swimming pool. It was known as Sleepy Lagoon, after a well-known melody played by band leader Harry James. The pit came to public attention when, after a gang fight involving the 38th Street Club, the body of gang member Juan Diaz was discovered on a nearby dirt road. In a flagrant violation of constitutional rights, police rounded up 22 of the 38th Street boys and charged every one of them with criminal conspiracy in the death of Diaz. Before it was over, about 600 Latino youth had been detained by police and questioned on suspicion of murder. The rationale of the authorities was evident: anyone who might have ties to pachuco gangs was a suspect in the murder.[3]

Though authorities were never able to link the altercation at Sleepy Lagoon with the murder—they had absolutely no tangible evidence—the press portrayed the 22 defendants as guilty hoodlums. The L.A. Sheriff's Department released a report concluding that Chicanos were "inherently violent" and—because they descended from Aztecs, who supposedly sacrificed thousands of victims every day—had an "utter disregard for life." Before LAPD Detective Mark Fuhrman's racist attitudes were exposed in the O.J. Simpson murder trial, LAPD Lieutenant Edward Ayres was in a class by himself. His written report to a 1942 grand jury was widely quoted. Ayres referred to the "inborn characteristic that has come down through the ages" that made young Mexicans in the city "let blood" in their gang wars. He said that since they respect nothing but violence and a tough hand, the only way to deal with their delinquency would be to sentence all of them to long jail terms or, as an option, military service.[1]

Throughout the trial, the defendants were not allowed to change their clothes or cut their hair, "for the purposes of identification." In early January 1943, with a salivating press reporting "the facts" of the trial, the district court found the Chicano youth guilty of crimes ranging from assault to first-degree murder.[2]

As headlines of the trial were carried across the country, anti-Mexican sentiment soared. Press reports depicted the zoot-suiters as sex criminals, delinquents and draft dodgers. Even the "Li'l Abner" Sunday comic strips demonized young Chicanos wearing zoot suits.

(In fact, comic books were a billion-dollar industry during the war, and common story lines included white American heroes wiping out everything that was culturally foreign. Racism and xenophobia were key elements in their success.)

The convictions were later overturned, thanks in large measure to the efforts of the Sleepy Lagoon Defense Committee, a collection of progressive and left-leaning organizations as well as some prominent Hollywood celebrities including Orson Welles, Anthony Quinn and Rita Hayworth. But the damage was done. Subsequent harassment by the police, who were doing the public's will in eliminating the scourge of the zoot-suiters, led to indiscriminate arrests and a newspaper-fueled atmosphere of racist violence. The worst was soon to follow.

The Sailor Riots

Tensions between young Chicanos in East Los Angeles and white military personnel on leave had been growing since the war began. Key military installations in Los Angeles—Terminal Island, the navy compounds where Dodger Stadium now sits and adjoining army facilities at Fort MacArthur—were in close proximity to Mexican American communities and served as temporary homes for thousands of sailors, many of whom spent their free time at the beaches or tourist attractions. Other sailors, though, roamed the nearby Chicano neighborhoods in large groups "looking for Spanish girls." They usually found trouble.

"They came into our community and took our hospitality for shit," said Lucy Rivera, whose father ran a club along Whittier Boulevard. "The navy people would act like they owned the place. My father told me how they would talk to him like he was some kind of servant. They asked him about the Mexican girls in the area and how much they cost. When they would get drunk, there would be trouble."[3]

Violence occurred throughout the spring of 1943, culminating in the riots that came to be known as the Zoot Suit Riots (perhaps more appropriately called the Sailor Riots), which were touched off on June 3 after a fight between off-duty sailors and local Chicanos. The sailors were chased out of the neighborhood, but later that night they returned, after spreading the word to their fellow sailors that the pachucos were "fair game" and that the police seemed willing to look the other way. For bored or anxious young servicemen about to be shipped off to war, the barrios would function as a kind of training ground.

The next evening, more than 200 sailors rampaged down Whittier Boulevard in the heart of East L.A., beating up young Chicanos and stripping off their zoot suits. Blacks and Filipinos who lived in the neighborhood or happened on the scene were also attacked. One Black man was pulled off a streetcar and one of his eyes gouged out with a knife. Fewer than half of all those attacked were actually wearing zoot suits.

On weekend leave from his station in San Diego, Miguel Feliciano was on his way to his family's house just off Whittier Boulevard. He had heard radio reports of fighting in the neighborhood, but shrugged them off as the "usual kinds of things that happened every now and again." When he got home, however, he couldn't believe what he heard and was soon to see. "I was flabbergasted that something like this could happen in my own home town," he said, many years later. "I knew there was discrimination and racism and all that. But I couldn't believe what I saw in some people's faces. And it wasn't just a bunch of drunk sailors either. I saw men who looked like they had just arrived from the hills, or from their big houses somewhere else."[4]

Over the next several days, apparently buoyed by police inaction and newspaper headlines suggesting that the sailors were heroes, more whites, including civilians, poured into the barrios. The navy lost control over several thousand servicemen. On the night of June 5, scores of them marched four abreast down the street yelling at Chicanos to take off their zoot suits or else. Sailors called their missions "landing parties," "taxicab brigades," "punitive expeditions," and "mopping up operations."[5]

But the press reported that the "zoot-suiters" were the real danger and headlines ("Zoot-Suit Gangsters Plan War on Navy") warned of an armed mob of 500 revenge-seeking pachucos ready for combat. That was enough to ensure an even larger turnout of whites the next couple of nights.

Rumors spread that the servicemen were committing rapes and other sexual assaults. "They weren't just rumors to me," said Juana Alvarez, who was thirteen at the time. "My best friend was attacked by some white sailors. They asked her if she had been in Tijuana the week before with them. Four of them grabbed her. I was the only one she told."[6]

On June 7, thousands of whites filled the streets between Main and Broadway, destroying property, breaking into bars and restaurants and dragging Chicanos into the street. White taxi drivers offered to take sailors and civilians alike into Chicano neighborhoods free of charge. Seven truckloads of sailors hurried to L.A. from their base in Las Vegas. A civilian crowd of more than 5,000 gathered in downtown, ready to follow circulated leaflet instructions in how to "de-zoot" a pachuco: "Grab a zooter. Take off his pants and frock coat and tear them up or burn them. Trim the 'Argentine ducktail' that goes with the screwy costume..." The press reported the violence as if it were the Los Angeles front of the war raging in Europe.[7]

"I remember my mom yelling at us [children] to stay inside," said George Valenzuela, who was only seven years old at the time. "My oldest brother was in the marines. I kept thinking how much I wish he was there to help protect my family. I thought that he could make the military people stop because he was kind of one of them. Now when I think about it, I figure that they probably would have gone after him too. It was a scary time."[8]

"My instinct was to fight back," Feliciano said, "but we felt pretty vulnerable and it looked like we wouldn't get help from the cops. Really, the cops, the cab drivers, the bus drivers, the city officials, everybody it seemed who was white was ready to help wipe us out."[9]

As vulnerable as many people in the community felt, there wasn't any lying down. Young Chicanos from East L.A. formed defense patrols, and when confronted with sailors, fought back and drove them out of the neighborhoods. Four sailors were cornered by a large group of pachucos and were severely beaten. Mothers and fathers stood on their front porches with rifles to protect their houses.

Returning Mexican American servicemen fought in the streets against whites who had the same uniforms on. "This was our community," said Osvaldo Ramirez. "I might have been a marine like some of those white boys who came up from El Toro (marine Base), but I was Mexican first. I wasn't going to just hide and let them come in here and tear up my people."[10]

The riots went on for more than a week. They spread into Pasadena, Long Beach and as far south as San Diego. The L.A. City Council quickly banned the wearing of zoot suits. L.A. Police arrested more than 600 young Chicanos, but only after dozens had been injured. Though no one was killed, there were cases of 12-year-olds being stripped naked and bloodied, their jaws broken and ribs cracked. Realizing that the police were not going to prevent the situation from getting worse, naval authorities finally declared the areas off limits to the military. Classified military documents later revealed that the navy thought it had a mutiny on its hands.

Media Racism and Complicity

"Zoot Suiters Learn Lesson in Fight with Servicemen," ran the headlines in the *Los Angeles Times.* Radio reports and editorials also praised the sailors and blamed the "violence-prone Mexicans." Investigative committees issued reports recommending punishment for the Chicanos involved. (One committee actually did blame the "disturbances" on white racism and media complicity—a "new" concept that is discovered each time fighting erupts in Los Angeles, only to be quickly forgotten.)

The Zoot Suit Riots in Los Angeles were not the only major clashes of the summer of 1943. In other towns—such as Evansville, Indiana, and Klamath Falls, Oregon—tiffs involving military and civilians were reported but were supposedly not racial in nature. Yet in other cities, racism was a key ingredient. In New York City and Philadelphia, police brutality touched off simmering tensions in Black communities. The worst rioting occurred on June 20, 1943, in Detroit, leaving 34 dead and hundreds wounded.

To most of America, these "disturbances" did not mean much in the larger context of war. Most felt that the "civility of the home front" was remarkable considering all the tension of the time. Even the ACLU remarked on how well "our democracy [could] maintain the essentials of liberty" while "we experienced no hysteria, no war-inspired mob violence, no pressure for suppressing dissent."[11] But it seemed clear enough to many people of color back on the home front that the "essentials of liberty" were reserved for whites.

In East L.A., the overall damage was relatively minor, but the attacks on the Chicano community had long-lasting effects. Mexican American youth were in many ways transformed. Feeling more "alien" than ever before, a good number of those attacked during the riots shaved their heads as a kind of badge of honor marking their rejection of victimization. They had survived white America's onslaught. When Mexican American soldiers returned home for good after the war, they found a community that had changed profoundly.

"Nothing was the same in my neighborhood after the riots," George Valenzeula says, more than fifty years later. "But that was kind of a good thing. We looked at them [whites] differently. We knew that they didn't like us, so we grew up thinking, to hell with them. We didn't need them either. We were going in another direction. A lot of us started calling ourselves 'Chicano.' We became active in community projects. We started to take pride in who we were. Maybe that's what the pachucos were doing back then, I don't know. But what happened in 1943 changed us forever."[12]

New community organizing efforts, like those started by the Community Service Organization (CSO), emerged in the aftermath of the confrontations. The CSO differed from other community-based efforts in that rather than just providing direct services, it was dedicated to grassroots community organizing around issues like police brutality, restricted housing, segregated schools, discriminatory employment practices and other inequitable treatment. The CSO helped train many young Mexican Americans in community organizing techniques, including Cesar Chavez, who would later go on to bigger battles.

Many contemporary observers of the Chicano movement of the 1960s and 1970s trace the origins of community consciousness to the events of the early 1940s. Sleepy Lagoon and the Zoot Suit Riots were the straws that broke the camel's back. The resulting ethnic and nationalist sentiments fueled organizing efforts that later blossomed in East L.A. high school walkouts protesting the lack of ethnic studies and general racism among school officials in the late

1960s and the Chicano Moratorium protesting the Vietnam War in 1970. After the zoot-suiters made history, the Chicano community was never the same.

NOTES

1. Meier and Rivera, *Readings on La Raza*, pp. 127–133.
2. Acuña, *Occupied America*, pp. 254–255.
3. Lucy Rivera, interview with author, San Diego State University, July 18, 1992.
4. Miguel Felíciano, interview with author, San Diego State University, July 18, 1992.
5. Mazón, *The Zoot Suit Riots*, pp. 78–79.
6. Juana Alvarez, interview with author, San Diego State University, July 26, 1992.
7. Mazón, p. 76.
8. George Valenzuela, interview with author, San Francisco, California, August 1993.
9. Ibid.
10. Osvaldo Ramirez, interview with author, San Diego State University, July 26, 1992.
11. Mazón, p. 54.
12. See footnote 8.

CHAPTER FOUR

"It's Our Union Too"

Mexican American Women Rescue the "Salt of the Earth" Strike

In the early 1950s, dissent was seldom expressed in bold ways, especially if it originated in communities of color. The reactionary mood of the country, exemplified by McCarthyism (the hysterical Congressional effort to ferret out Communists led by Senator Joseph McCarthy) served to quiet potential outbursts of protest against injustice. One important exception can be found in the events that took place in Hanover, New Mexico from October 1950 to January 1952. In what has become known as the "Salt of the Earth" strike, because of the classic and controversial film by that name that it inspired, Mexican Americans, and particularly Chicana women, made history.

The fight in New Mexico was more than a typical labor battle. The Mine Mill and Smelter Workers Union (Mine-Mill), Local 890, with a predominantly Mexican American membership, went up against the powerful Empire Zinc Mining Company in an effort to win better pay and working conditions, but the strike is more importantly remembered as a campaign against both racism and sexism. The favorable treatment accorded white mine workers at Empire Zinc and throughout the industry made organizing along racial lines necessary. The fact that Mexican American women exerted their leadership and organizing potential during the strike makes it a chapter worth retelling.

The "Other" Workers

By the 1950s, Mexican Americans, most of them born in the U.S., made up about one-half of New Mexico's population. Racism had always been a part of their lives, but after World War II, when whites from Texas arrived to work in the oil fields and in the mines, the problem deepened. Competition for jobs and an unequal wage system that paid Mexican Americans on average about half of what whites earned caused much friction. Seen as socially and racially inferior, Mexican Americans, especially those who were darker, suffered many of the indignities that plagued Blacks living in the segregated South.

Mexicans had long worked in the copper mines of New Mexico and had just as long been struggling against racial discrimination, first from the Spanish, then from elite Mexican absentee owners and finally from U.S. companies like Empire Zinc. As early as 1915, Mexican miners, joined by some Anglo workers, conducted strikes against the decidedly anti-union companies. Cooperation between Chicano and white miners was short-lived, however, because of the company's success in fostering racial divisions among the workers. Organizing in the 1930s and 1940s was difficult. Benigño Montéz remembers:

> We had to have meetings at midnight after shift work...There was always company officers watching to see what was going on, so we had to have meetings in different places. They fought organizing...They would say, "You've been off too much" and they'd fire you. But that was not why they fired you. They fired you because you were active organizing. Other miners kept on getting drunk and laying off and having absenteeism, but they were not active. They weren't fired. It was the active guys, the miners who wanted to improve working conditions—the company was after them all the time.[1]

In Grant County, where the Empire Zinc Company mined, Mexican Americans were half the population in 1950, but they were nearly absent from the voter rolls. Most had dropped out of high school to find work in the fields or mines to help their families survive. Despite a brief period of excitement when Chicano GI's returned from fighting in World War II, hopes of a better life soon were diminished by the reality of a racially tiered system favoring whites. In fact, business in Grant County was run no differently than in some of the counties in Mississippi. The copper companies were able to segregate workers even to the point where payroll lines read "Anglo-American Males" and "Other Employees," meaning everyone else, including Mexicans, Blacks, Filipinos, and of course all women.

During World War II, most unions took a no-strike pledge in order to keep the country's business going, but the patriotic management-labor harmony existed only superficially and would be shattered by the end of the war. The reasons were clear enough: in places like Hanover, New Mexico and throughout the Southwest, where dramatic disparities in wages and treatment of workers existed, particularly by race, militant organizing was sure to follow.

Difficult Days for Labor

The dawn of the 1950s also presented other issues. The U.S. government had started toward a Cold War with the Soviet Union and, domestically, that translated into harsh measures against any person or organization deemed left-wing, progressive, and, most of all, Communist. The Taft-Hartley Act, passed in 1947, placed a variety of limitations on union activities, including denying government certification to unions whose officers and members failed to sign non-Communist affidavits. At the same time, companies that did business in mineral resources like copper and zinc were looking to extend the great profits made during the war years. They would need to keep control over their workers, especially those with strong unions backing them up. It wasn't an easy time to be a union like Mine-Mill Local 890.

Mine-Mill's predecessor was the Western Federation of Miners (WFM), co-founders in 1905 of the Industrial Workers of the World, known as the "Wobblies," which earlier in the century had led workers in many of the labor conflicts in the western part of the country. But in the early 1950s, a depression in the metals industry weakened the union, as more than half of the 2,000 mine employees in Grant County were laid off. Exacerbating their problems, much of the union's support was stripped when Mine-Mill was expelled from the accommodationist Congress of Industrial Organizations (CIO) for being too radical and many of its Mexican American members were harassed by Immigration and Naturalization Service agents. The mining industry's hand could be seen at work behind these setbacks; it was clearly out to break the back of the union.

Local 890's membership, especially those who were Chicano, had long complained about differences in wages that Chicano laborers, muckers and miners earned doing often dangerous, backbreaking underground work compared to the wages paid to surface workers and craftsmen, jobs filled mostly by whites.

In addition, Mexican American workers, including those working in Empire Zinc's mines, suffered the humiliation of segregated facilities and work tasks. The blatant segregation of separate payroll lines, washrooms, toilet facilities and housing were all common practice in the mines of Grant County. Mexican American housing, for the most part, did not have indoor plumbing; when the union asked Empire Zinc to install facilities and negotiate further on rent and other matters, the company ignored the requests.

In this context, Local 890 of Mine-Mill formally presented a series of demands to Empire in 1950, among them full payment for "collar-to-collar" work, meaning compensation for all the time the miner spent underground, paid holidays, an end to separate and unequal facilities, elimination of the no-strike clause in their contract and, in general, regional parity with other organized miners, who were mostly white.

Local 890 did not consider their demands excessive. Yet it soon became evident that Empire Zinc—which had made record profits the preceding two years despite the industry fall-off and was doing even better as the demand for zinc rose with the outbreak of the Korean War—would not move on these matters. In fact, the company refused to negotiate at all, and the union could only conclude that management's aim was to break the union. The company disagreed. "We are not trying to destroy this union," said Empire Zinc's chief negotiator Richard Berresford. "We are trying to give it proper leadership."

The acquiescence displayed by mainstream unionism did not mean that all organized workers would indulge the McCarthys and the corporate leaders. In fact, Mine-Mill continued its class and race-conscious stance, much to the chagrin of Empire Zinc and local officials. With the first rumblings of a strike, the company and the media began to red-bait and discredit Local 890 and accused some of its leaders—people like Clint and Virginia Jencks and others—of being Communists. In fact, as was common in those days, some of

Local 890's leaders were admitted Communists, but it was clear from the beginning that the rank-and-file of the union and most of its leadership were more interested in changing conditions than in advancing political ideology.

Local 890 voted to strike in October 1950, and showed their impressive organizational abilities by supporting striking workers with weekly funds and mobilizing a large contingent of pickets. Still, for seven months negotiations went nowhere, despite the fact that the plant wasn't operable—and costing the company tens of thousands of dollars daily—even after the union dropped all but the most crucial demands.

Then, in early June 1951, the company announced that it would reopen the mine, leading 890 to call for picket line reinforcements. On June 12, the county sheriff's office helped escort strikebreakers down the road to the plant. The pickets met them and refused to let them pass. Twelve of the pickets, including leaders like Clint Jencks, Jose Carillo and fifty-year-old Elvira Molano (one of the few women who had marched with the men) were arrested. Later, the District Court handed down an injunction making any further union picketing illegal and the marchers subject to arrest.

The Women Take the Wheel

The strike would have ended there with a company victory and not much for the historians to write about, but a heated all-night union meeting on the night of the 12th produced a new strategy. With much hesitation on the part of the men in the union, the "ladies' auxiliary" of Local 890 argued convincingly for their participation. Technically not union members and therefore not covered by the court order, the women would march as pickets the next day.

The women's group had received an official union charter the year before in order to "enlist the aid of all miners' families to further the principles of trade unionism." Though the statement implied that the women were to be actively involved in the affairs and direction of the local, in reality they remained relegated to planning social events like dances and bingo, making enchilada dinners and taking care of children. In the first several months of the strike, the auxiliary had worked at distributing flyers and composing scripts for the union's radio ads, but they were still very much in the background, consumed by their household duties. Now they were about to take center stage.

Mariana Ramirez captained the picket line and divided the women into two teams of eight, one for each entrance to the mine. The all-female pickets — most of whom were the wives and daughters of the male union members—prevented scab workers from entering the mill. Emboldened by that first day's success, the leadership of the auxiliary, Ramirez, Virginia Chacón, Anita Torres, Braulia Velásquez and others, decided that the picket line should continue. In full-page newspaper ads, Empire Zinc condemned the union for exposing women and children to the hazards of the picket line.

But if the company was worried about the safety of the women, they might have thought better of ordering their police force, which incidentally was the county's police force as well, into the picket line. On June 16, newly deputized officers, most of whom were white and overtly hostile to the brown-skinned people resisting to their faces, charged the line. A couple of tear-gas canisters were tossed into the crowds and sixty-two people were arrested—45 women and 17 children, including a twenty-nine-day-old baby. All were taken to a cramped jail which had a capacity for only about twenty. One of the striking women, Virginia Chacón remembers:

> I myself didn't know what a jail was. I didn't know what it looked like, and, of course, we were all nervous in there, after we saw the rest of the women in there, and these paid gunmen register-ing us, and they said we have a choice of either staying in jail or going back home but we were not allowed to go back to the picket lines. We all responded at the same time we would not go home, we would go back to the picket lines and help our strikers, help our union members.[3]

It's Our Union, Too

Even without promising to stay off the picket lines, the women were soon released. Their resolve strengthened when they learned that they had made national headlines. The picket lines continued with the women chanting, "No les dejen pasar," or "Don't let them pass." The growing militancy of the women was summed up by

Molano when she said that Empire Zinc and the sheriff's office "failed to realize that we women are a part of this fight...and we shall carry this fight to the victorious finish."[4]

Arrests and jailings also continued. So did the violence. Empire Zinc offered a half-day's wages to scab workers who tried to break the women's picket line. Police reinforced the scabs by beating some of the women and allowing cars to be used as battering rams. Two women were hit by cars on one occasion. But the women stayed on the lines and let themselves be carted off to jail. "They arrested so many of us they finally couldn't fill the jail with any more," said Virginia Derr Chambers, a wife of one of the Mine-Mill union leaders.[5]

At home the women also faced the sexism of some of their less-than-supportive husbands. "What we need is more help from the men on the many jobs off the line," said Elena Montoya. "We need more help on the jobs we cannot do at home while we are doing this job."[6]

Virginia Chacón remembers,

> We asked the men to bring their wives [to union meetings], and sometimes they wouldn't, and we'd go visit the lady. And she'd tell us why she wouldn't participate—that her husband would say that ladies shouldn't belong to an organization—just do women's things. So we'd talk to her, and finally we'd convince her...I felt that if Johnny [her husband] was going to be active in the union, why shouldn't I? What's good for the goose is good for the gander. We felt that the union is not for the men only, it's our union too...We felt that if our husbands were going to belong to the union, we should do something about it too.[7]

Some men had to put their pride in check and deal with the reality. "I hate to be calling her a wife now," said Ernesto Velasquez of his wife, Braulia. "She's the boss of the family. It so happened the 13th of June she took over the household. We have a little baby and she said you go home and wash the dishes and change the diapers. That puts me in an embarrassing position. I have washed the dishes and I have swept the house, but one thing I cannot get myself to do and that is change a diaper."[8]

Mine-Mill organizer Clint Jencks understood the importance of women getting involved in organizing and in working the lines.

> We needed unity among the workers, but I found out that we

didn't even have unity in our families. [Most of the men didn't include the women in their discussions about what to do with the strike.] But it is the women who have the responsibility of taking the meager paychecks and trying to spread them over all the needs of the household and the kids. All of a sudden, the man comes home from work one day and says, 'We're gonna strike. There's gonna be no income.' What would naturally be the reaction of a woman when she's been excluded? The man doesn't even conceive of the problem. I moved from thinking it was a union struggle to realizing it was a struggle of the whole people.[9]

Solidarity was always evident on the strike lines and the men eventually played supporting roles, but the union and the community would have to face up to its treatment and expectations of the women who proved to be the backbone of the struggle. The initial day of picketing turned into seven months of the women keeping the strike alive.

Despite the fact that the images of women and children being arrested and harassed by company goons made Empire Zinc look like the bad guy, the union, in fact, was losing the public relations battle. This was mainly because the local newspapers, including the influential *Grant County Daily Press*, took the company's side. The *Daily Press*'s racist editor, Todd Ely, told the Mexican American community that the reason for their "ill success" lay in their own shortcomings. "Mexico, of course, is poverty stricken," he wrote, "because its early settlers lost their identity in a mestizo melting pot that lowered the general level of culture to a point little above that of the swarming aborigines."[10]

Knitting Needles and Chili Powder

As the strike continued, the violence intensified. Every time the company attempted to use force to clear the line, the women retaliated by throwing rocks and even chili powder into the eyes of strikebreakers or newly deputized goons. "Everybody had a gun, except us," said Mariana Ramirez. "We had knitting needles. We had safety pins. We had straight pins. We had chili peppers. And we had rotten eggs."[11]

In late August 1951, things finally got completely out of hand. On August 22, several cars were driven into pickets, injuring a woman and organizer Bob Hollowwa, one of the few men who had encouraged the activism of the women. In retaliation, a crowd of pickets and their supporters nearly destroyed one car and beat up a couple of the goons.

The next day would be known as the "Bloody 23rd." The company and its strikebreakers met with the sheriff and made plans to shut down the strike using whatever force was necessary. Several cars lurched into the picket lines that day, seriously injuring Rachel Juarez, Consuela Martinez and sixty-four-year-old Bersabe Yguado. One of the deputies fired his gun into the crowd, hitting a union worker who had just come back from duty in Korea. The *Daily Press* condemned the union for starting the fight and prominently featured company ads under the title, "What Happens When a Mob Runs Wild?"[12]

But the union and the women, who had proved to be the toughest of all, refused to back down. Worried about the negative publicity New Mexico was getting, the state governor finally intervened on behalf of the company and issued orders prohibiting blocking the road leading to the mine. The workers and the women on the line simply could not afford to do time in the state penitentiary, with its longer sentences. From this vulnerable position, the union agreed to arbitration.

The company had also been battered by the protracted strike. It had lost big money and agreed it would be easier to end the fight as well. Though they were loathe to admit it, the company gave in to many of Local 890's key demands, including substantial wage increases that made the hourly pay among the highest in the district and some very important benefits, particularly in health and accident insurance and holiday and vacation pay. The union also won the right to negotiate rates for new jobs and for workers to use grievance procedures during their probationary period.

Though the new contract provided for the continuing employment of some of the strikebreakers, it also allowed all strikers to return to work with full seniority rights. Even though not spelled out in the contract, the workers and their families soon discovered that the company would install modern indoor plumbing in their homes. On the negative side, several members of the union had to serve prison sentences of several months and many more had to pay costly fines.

Perhaps most significant in the larger sense was the fact that for the families of Hanover, a new sense of pride and possibility had emerged from challenging the powerful company.

Mexican American women, though still faced with resistance from a traditional community, proved they were as capable of struggle as the men. They, along with the larger Chicano community, realized as never before their untapped strength, a full decade ahead of the civil rights and women's liberation movements. Their efforts, forever immortalized in the film *Salt of the Earth*,[13] provide vivid lessons to future generations fighting the good fight in difficult times.

NOTES

1. Wilson and Rosenfelt, *Salt of the Earth*, p. 114.

2. Cargill, "Empire and Opposition," p. 241.

3. Ibid, p. 208.

4. Wilson and Rosenfelt, p. 120.

5. Cargill, p. 233.

6. Ibid, p. 205.

7. Wilson and Rosenfelt, p. 137.

8. Cargill, p. 244.

9. Wilson and Rosenfelt, p. 136.

10. Cargill, p. 213.

11. Wilson and Rosenfelt, p. 140.

12. Cargill, pp. 228–230.

13. The film *Salt of the Earth* was made shortly after the strike, using both dramatic reenactment and documentary footage from the strike. The red-baiting of the times was so intense that the three artists responsible for making the film—Herbert Biberman, Paul Jerrico and Michael Wilson—had to go underground much of the time during production and after release of the film. "We were hounded by denunciations on the floor of Congress and by columnists," said Paul Jerrico in an interview on "The News Hour" (PBS-TV, October 24, 1997). "The public was told we were making a new weapon for Russia. Our star [Rosaura Revueltas] was arrested and deported." The film was banned in the U.S. when it appeared in 1953.

CHAPTER FIVE

Affirmative Action from the Grassroots

African Americans Demand Jobs in San Francisco

In July 1964 an editorial in the *San Francisco Chronicle* proclaimed, "unlike other areas of the country, civil rights principles and equal opportunity are not in question in San Francisco." The editors apparently didn't bother to read their own newspaper. On the front page of the same day's *Chronicle* was a news story about a mass demonstration outside the corporate offices of the Bank of America, the biggest and most powerful bank in the world.

The demonstrators, according to the report, were demanding that "Jim Crow Must Go in San Francisco," a familiar cry of the Civil Rights Movement, which was then in full swing. Despite the surface similarity, however, the struggle in San Francisco was not about segregation or voting rights, as it was in African American communities across the South. Faced with a period of deep unemployment in Black communities, organizers and activists in San Francisco built on the national momentum of the Civil Rights Movement to launch what was essentially a grassroots political fight for economic development and jobs. While activists of all colors were streaming to Alabama, Mississippi and Washington, D.C. in the early 1960s for mass demonstrations and marches to protest continued segregation of Blacks, San Francisco organizers were aiming to crack open the job market for African Americans. It was one of the earliest fights for affirmative action and it came from the streets, not the halls of Congress.

Today, more than thirty years later, urban Black America is once again in the throes of severe economic dislocation and high unemployment (and affirmative action programs are on the chopping block). While political elites in San Francisco fight over ever-decreasing budgets and community leaders expend enormous energies to build a few units of low-income housing or guarantee a handful of jobs on a construction project, the African American community is declining in power, resources and numbers. Few analysts believe that the limited economic development programs currently in place can reverse this situation, and a growing chorus of voices is calling for a new civil rights struggle, one that, as Manning Marable puts it, "extend[s] democratic principles from the social and political system into the structures of the economy, making a job a human right."[1]

If there is going to be a new civil rights struggle focusing on employment and the economy of the inner city, organizers would do well to review how the movement for jobs developed three decades ago.

Going to the Grassroots

"We went to the grassroots," remembers Oba T'Shaka, who was a key organizer in the San Francisco movement for jobs in the early 1960s, "and they said that the biggest problem was the fact that they couldn't find work. In the early sixties, there were no Blacks downtown except those shining shoes and sweeping streets. The formation of the movement here was in that context."[2]

T'Shaka, who now teaches in the Black Studies Department at San Francisco State University, was then known as Bill Bradley. In the early 1960s, he was local chair of the Congress of Racial Equality (CORE), which was then the cutting-edge organization of the San Francisco Civil Rights Movement. CORE and other civil rights organizations built a movement for jobs demanding that major San Francisco employers not only end discrimination against African Americans and other people of color, but also instate specific hiring quotas. In the course of a few years, an organized, unified and militant movement in San Francisco signed more than 260 separate agreements with city employers, resulting in thousands of new jobs for African Americans and a significant boost to the community.

The jobs campaigns of 1963 and 1964 had a single goal: To force supermarkets, hotels, restaurants, auto dealers, utility companies, department stores, transit lines and banks to make immediate and substantial efforts to hire African Americans. Major demonstrations for jobs, unparalleled in other areas of the country, placed San Francisco squarely on the map of civil rights hot spots in the early 1960s. Pickets, demonstrations, boycotts, "shop-ins" and other creative tactics were used to persuade large employers that they had to make good on liberal San Francisco's promise of equal opportunity and greater equality in hiring.

War Brings the Promise of Jobs

During World War II, as the national economy shifted to meet the demands of war, a surplus of jobs in the shipbuilding industry opened up opportunities for many who had been previously considered untrainable and unemployable. According to Douglas Daniels, author of *Pioneer Urbanites,* a book about Blacks in San Francisco, the demand for labor in California was a beacon call to African Americans in the South:

> Most of the newcomers migrated from the western regions of the South—Texas, Louisiana and Arkansas. Henry Kaiser, the industrialist who built ships for the war, 'brought Blacks here from all over the South—every state—and he brought them in train loads. He brought one to three train loads every day for six months.'[3]

The San Francisco Bay Area, an embarkation point for the U.S. military heading for the Pacific Theater, became a shipbuilding center. Henry J. Kaiser built shipyards in Richmond, Oakland, Vallejo and Sausalito; Bechtel established Marinship in Sausalito and the U.S. government bought the Bethlehem Shipbuilding Company at Hunters Point in San Francisco. In the 1940s alone, the African American population in the Bay Area jumped more than 600 percent until there were well over 40,000 Blacks there by the end of World War II.

While many African Americans in San Francisco prospered during the war, they were nonetheless still subject to discrimination. For example, most labor unions refused union votes to Blacks even though they paid dues. And in 1944, nearly half of the 100 leading San Francisco industries still did not employ a single African American.

Nevertheless, before the end of the war, Bay Area shipyards employed more than 300,000 new workers, including many of the

Blacks who had moved to the area. As they sent for family and friends still in the South, the Black population increased.

When the war ended, the great demand for shipbuilding subsided. Moreover, many whites returning from military service settled in San Francisco, increasing the competition for jobs. When the shipyards and other waterfront jobs closed, the rate of unemployment in the Black community soared. The era of prosperity for Blacks came to a grinding halt.

The tremendous migration of Black war workers to the Bay Area had created an equally tremendous demand for housing. Considered "temporaries," African Americans in San Francisco were placed in large, government-subsidized housing tracts in Hunters Point and in vacant housing in the Fillmore District, an area recently evacuated by Japanese and Japanese American citizens forced into government concentration camps during the war.

Housing patterns became distinctly racially segregated. As Blacks moved into the Fillmore and nearby Western Addition areas, whites left for areas further from the city's center. Hunters Point, which had been nearly all white in 1940, became 90 percent Black by 1970. Later, housing restrictions keeping Blacks out of some neighborhoods led to some embarrassing press when it was discovered that baseball star Willie Mays had been denied housing in a white, affluent section of the city.

Even Herb Caen, the popular *Chronicle* columnist and San Francisco booster, had to admit,

> The Negro "problem" is very much with the city, too. The Negro population has grown tenfold since World War II, but San Francisco, for all its vaunted tolerance, has moved slowly to meet the challenge that this presents. The Negro, now representing one-tenth of the city's population, is largely restricted to a single section of substandard old housing—centering on and radiating from Fillmore Street—and the ills implicit in such a situation are clearly to be seen: de facto segregation in the schools, inequitable job opportunities, crime out of proportion to the population, mass picketing and demonstrations.[4]

A Japanese Protestant minister observed in 1962 that the racism directed against the Japanese American community since relocation had been redirected to a large degree. "I suspect," he said, "that we have been bailed out by the Negroes. They moved in and frightened the whites, who then found that we Japanese weren't so bad after all. They could stop hating us and start hating the Negroes."[5]

Built-in Racism, San Francisco-Style

As institutional discrimination flowered, Manning Marable writes, "Blacks began to demand the inclusion of special economic reforms within the overall goals of the civil rights struggle. It was no victory for Black men to be allowed to sit in a formerly white-only theater or to rent hotel accommodation which had been segregated, when they had no jobs."[6] While the creation of Black neighborhoods and communities resulted in thriving social institutions (churches, nightclubs, restaurants and cabarets), economically and politically, Black San Franciscans were being shut out as the Civil Rights Movement appeared on the horizon.

African Americans did not find much solace with the unions either. With the notable exception of the progressive International Longshoreman's and Warehousemen's Union, most local trade unions systematically kept Black San Franciscans out in the post-World War II downsizing cold.

White reaction could be hostile, both on an institutional level and a personal one. One Employment Service official said, "I just hope that the Negroes will go back to Texas and take the whole damned race problem with them."[7] The most frequent response from local firms and unions was that San Francisco's African Americans lacked the education necessary to qualify for higher-level positions. In fact, one did not need a college degree to serve hamburgers, take reservations, update a bank account and the like. And study after study in the mid-to-late 1950s pointed to the fact that African Americans who did have jobs were earning far less than their white counterparts, even when both were performing the same task with the same amount of educational experience.

By the late 1950s, the Southern Civil Rights Movement was in the news every day, inspiring many Black San Franciscans, who were facing a crisis of deepening joblessness and wage discrimination, to call for improved conditions. Local mainstream (white) media establishments were not entirely ignorant of this mood. In 1963, a *San Francisco Chronicle* article reported that because San Francisco "has failed dismally to learn to live with [Negroes], only increasingly tense racial conflict—even racial clashes—lies ahead." Reporting that the general Black unemployment rate was nearly forty percent, five times that of whites living and working in the city, the *Chronicle* commented, "Negroes are frequently refused employment [even] in jobs with which their race has been identified since slave days."[8]

Southern Sparks Catch Fire

The movement for jobs in San Francisco grew out of community mobilization in solidarity with southern-based struggles for desegregation and voting rights.

"There couldn't have been a San Francisco movement without the southern movement," T'Shaka said. "Basically, the southern struggle was the launching pad, the initial thrust that set off sparks everywhere else. But there were different circumstances there and here. Birmingham started moving on jobs but most of that effort focused around eliminating segregation. Up here, we dealt with de facto segregation, particularly in housing. But the immediate issue, the bread and butter issue, was [the lack of] jobs."[6]

The San Francisco branch of CORE, moribund since the 1940s, was reorganized in 1960, thanks mainly to the efforts of community activists Ella Hill Hutch and Bob Slattery. Soon, CORE developed into a small but active cadre of organizers, including T'Shaka.

In July 1963 civil rights organizations sponsored a mass rally at the San Francisco Civic Center in solidarity with African Americans who were battling firehoses and police dogs in Birmingham, Alabama. But the focus soon shifted to local issues.

Later that month, CORE member Wilfred Ussery returned from Birmingham where he had spent a month learning about the movement in the South. Ussery and the rest of CORE began meeting with NAACP members, the Negro American Labor Council, the Bayview-Hunters Point Citizen Committee and the San Francisco Council of Negro Women. Together, these organizations joined under the umbrella heading of the United Freedom Movement (UFM).

"We in San Francisco CORE went into the pool halls, the beauty parlors and everywhere else where the grassroots were," T'Shaka recalls. "We organized around everyday Black folks' needs."[10]

On July 28, 1963, UFM co-chairpersons Dr. Thomas ("Nat") Burbridge and Ardath Nichols announced the UFM's goal of "complete equality for San Francisco Negroes, with particular emphasis on employment" and demanded the city and local businesses meet with the UFM to set out a plan. Surprising not only city officials but also moderate NAACP leaders, Burbridge called for a militant response from the Black community should negotiations break down:

> I don't mean negotiations for months either, I mean weeks—and a very few weeks. But if they fail, [we will have to employ] the sheer, naked, unrobed, undressed manipulation of power. This is ordinarily accomplished by the manipulation of money. The Negro community is the poor community, therefore, all we can do is interfere with the normal flow of money in San Francisco by demonstrations, boycotts and picket lines. We've got to really hurt somebody in the pocketbook.[9]

The goal was to obtain specific agreements that spelled out immediate numerical increases in positions for African Americans and other people of color. When employers failed to be persuaded in meetings with UFM leaders, they quickly became the target of an organized protest campaign.

The Mel's Drive-In Pickets

In the fall of 1963, the Direct Action Group (DAG), led by Art Sheridan, found there were almost no Blacks working for the popular San Francisco restaurant chain, Mel's Drive-In.

On October 19, DAG members picketed three Mel's Drive-Ins. Mel's owner, Harold Dobbs, a San Francisco Supervisor who was at the time the leading candidate to succeed George Christopher as the city's mayor, called the protest "politically contrived" by his Democratic opponent John F. Shelley.

DAG members, who made clear that the protests would continue every day until their demands were met, denied that they were pawns of Shelley. In reality, they had recognized the opportunity to thrust the issue of race and employment into the political mix as the election neared. This tactic was especially important as both candidates had pledged to keep the "race issue" out of the election.

The local white news media didn't pay much attention to the pickets at first. But the *Chronicle,* the biggest paper in the city and the one most aggressively endorsing Dobbs' candidacy, finally gave them some press when demonstrators picketed Dobbs' home just days before the election. Dobbs was livid. He maintained that he believed in equal opportunity for everyone, but wouldn't be "pushed around" by demands of "special rights or privileges for anyone, or any group."

Meanwhile, in the biggest demonstration, sixty-four people were arrested outside the largest of the restaurants, many carrying pickets with the slogan, "I'll have a freedomburger please." Two nights later, as the candidates were preparing their final appeals to voters, another forty-eight were arrested in what was termed a "wild melee" inside the same restaurant. As many of the protesters were white college students, the local media characterized them as bored and spoiled Marxist dupes. Amidst chanting and singing protesters pounding on tables, Mel's manager Jack Everett called police. When they came, he went to each protester and asked if they had anything to order; when they responded that they only wanted "freedom and jobs for Negroes," police arrested them and hauled them off.[12]

In Dobbs' final appeal to the "good and reasonable people of San Francisco," he remarked that the demonstrations were creating "another Birmingham atmosphere" in the city. "If [Shelley] gets elected," Dobbs said, "then San Francisco would indeed become another Birmingham." The statement backfired; Shelley was elected mayor the next night.[13]

But the election results did not translate into quiet on the picket front. After a two-day moratorium on demonstrations, picketing in front of the largest Mel's resumed, this time with participation from the NAACP's Burbridge (who was UFM chair) and other Black leaders. The management of the restaurant had to admit that the actions were having an affect. "Usually we have about 200 people either inside or eating in their cars at this time," lamented Everett, "I can count only 10 now."[14]

Finally, Mel's ownership and management sat down with the Black leadership to negotiate a settlement. With the threat of renewed and enlarged demonstrations that would expand to include Berkeley restaurants owned by Dobbs if the demands of immediate and substantial hiring of Blacks were not met, Mel's negotiators proposed as a solution filling "the next 10 to 20 positions" with Negroes, far short of what the UFM was calling for.

After more threats of demonstrations, Mel's gave in and signed a comprehensive nondiscriminatory hiring agreement at all 13 restaurants in the chain and pledged to begin a training school for Black workers. The settlement, which included provisions for immediate hiring at all the restaurants, was read to about 200 demonstrators just before they were about to resume picketing.

The Lucky "Shop-Ins"

With the exception of a CORE campaign in 1948, which had netted three jobs for Blacks at a San Francisco Lucky supermarket, not much had been done to address the gross disparity in employment representation at the 60 Lucky stores around the Bay Area. Then, in late 1963, the UFM and Lucky signed an agreement for increased Black presence in the stores' workforce. But over the next four months, Lucky hired only 18 Blacks out of 320 total new hires. Overall, fewer than one percent of all Lucky employees were Black.

Meanwhile, work on the East Coast was providing inspiration. In late 1963, the National CORE, and a committee representing local New York City CORE chapters, NAACP branches and Puerto Rican groups had won major concessions from the A&P grocery chain, in which A&P agreed to hire more than two hundred Blacks and Puerto Ricans over the next two years. In essence, A&P had agreed to hire only people of color for two years.

Soon thereafter, San Francisco CORE and the Baptist Ministers Union—representing San Francisco churches with a total membership of 40,000 people, most of them African American—announced they would be pressuring all the stores in the Lucky chain to increase employment of Blacks substantially. In response, Lucky announced that it would not "engage in reverse discrimination."

On February 17, 1964, CORE members stood outside one Lucky store picketing and singing protest songs. Inside the store, however, a new tactic was being used. Termed a "shop-in" by T'Shaka, CORE demonstrators loaded shopping carts with groceries and then abandoned them at the checkout stand, saying, "That's too much money," or "I'll have more money to pay you when you hire more Negroes." In some cases, demonstrators brought the carts to the checkout station but purchased only a pack of bubble gum. After an hour of such demonstrations, police were called and the "shoppers" dispersed.

CORE's action continued for nine days. One Lucky manager, Arden Grauman, reported that, despite the large crowd inside the store and the busy ringing of the cash register, "we didn't do any business to amount to anything." Groups of fraternity and sorority members from UC Berkeley attempted to help the "besieged" stores by putting items back on shelves, but Lucky upper management reported "substantial losses" nevertheless. The San Francisco police were frustrated that they couldn't "lock these people up" because the "gutless Lucky management" wouldn't press charges.[15]

On February 28, Lucky caved in and agreed to a comprehensive hiring agreement with CORE. The specifics of the agreement were not made public, but it was later reported that it guaranteed the hiring of up to 75 Blacks among 155 new clerks in the following five months. In fact, Lucky had agreed to hire only people of color (including "Orientals" and "Latin Americans") at Lucky stores for an entire year.

In 1960, CORE membership had been four-fifths white, but following the Lucky campaign and under T'Shaka's leadership, Black community support increased. It was helped by the fact that CORE had established offices in the Fillmore District, the political and cultural heart of Black San Francisco. Bolstered by the Lucky campaign and galvanized by intensive recruitment in the Black community, San Francisco CORE became predominately Black and decidedly more militant in future campaigns.

Victory at the Palace

In mid-February, 1964, the local news media reported that San Francisco's hotel and restaurant industry had reaped record-breaking profits from recent convention and tourist business. The opulent Sheraton Palace Hotel was featured as particularly successful.

Yet San Francisco's African Americans were barely to be found among the workforce of the city's lucrative hotel and restaurant industry. In the city's early days, many of its Black "pioneer urbanites" had been employed in the hotels and restaurants as bellhops, waiters, cooks, maids and the like. But with the Panic of 1873 and the deep and prolonged national recession that followed, Black San Franciscans were forced out of many jobs by boycotting whites who felt that they should not be jobless while Blacks held decent-paying positions. That era's economic distress, coupled with subsequent decades of hostile and protectionist white union racism and large-scale employment discrimination, effectively kept Blacks out of San Francisco's downtown workforce for close to a century.

But on March 1, 1964—the very day the Lucky/CORE agreements were announced—an organized picket of the Sheraton Palace Hotel began. The Ad Hoc Committee to End Discrimination, led by 18-year-old San Francisco State student Tracy Sims (one of the few Blacks in the organization), marched through the ritzy hotel lobby, much to the surprise and consternation of wealthy tourists and native San Franciscans. The Ad Hoc Committee listed as its biggest demand that the hotel, which had only nineteen Black workers out of more than 550 employees, begin "immediately hiring a reasonable number" of Blacks. The Sheraton Palace insisted that the numbers of "minority representation" in their workforce was greater than was being alleged. But the hotel was counting Greeks and Armenians as members of minority groups and therefore ignoring the claim of bias against Blacks.

The following day, as picketing continued in defiance of a court injunction, more than eighty demonstrators, including Black comedian Dick Gregory, were arrested and taken to jail. The police response was swift and often brutal. After watching his fellow pickets being dragged to waiting paddy wagons by their feet, their heads bouncing off the pavement, Gregory remarked on national news, "This is as brutal as anything I've seen in the South." The effect of the police repression, according to Thomas Dammann, Jr., one of the participants in the demonstration, was actually helpful to the campaign since "it drew many more people to our ranks."[16]

Sheraton Palace manager Morgan Smith announced that the hotel would not be pressured into make special hiring arrangements "because this hotel does not and will not tolerate discrimination in hiring." Mayor Shelley worried that "some of these demonstrators are just young kids who are going out and having a ball." Shelley remarked in a packed press conference that the pickets could "do great harm to the cause of better race relations in San Francisco" and that Gregory's comments about police brutality were unfounded. "I think Gregory still thinks he's in the South—he'll find that the attitudes in San Francisco aren't anything like feelings there."[17]

Four days later, on March 6, more than 1,500 protesters surrounded the Palace; about 500 of them went inside the lobby for a sit-in. Irate hotel guests, disgusted with the pickets' visible use of slogans such as "Jim Crow Must Go in San Francisco" and "Freedom Now," commented bitterly that "it's disgraceful that the city would permit so many misfits to demonstrate." The next day, even more demonstrators packed the lobby and surrounded the outside of the hotel, leading to a San Francisco record of 167 arrests. News accounts spoke of "bedlam" in the Palace, once "celebrated as the Bonanza Inn of the Comstock Lode era and symbol of elegance that catered to presidents and the potentates of the world."

In the wake of the massive demonstrations and three-inch headline publicity from the local dailies, negotiations got underway. While hundreds of protesters camped inside the lobby in the early hours of March 8, the Palace management was faced with conflicting demands from the activists and the powerful Hotel Owners Association (HOA). The HOA, which represented thirty-three of the city's biggest hotels, feared that if the Palace gave in, the other hotels would be forced into similar agreements. They were right. The hotel could no longer bear the publicity of massive racial protests; nor could the Owners Association.

That afternoon, an excited Tracy Sims and other members of the negotiating committee addressed the demonstrators: "We came here trying to end the discriminatory hiring practices at the Sheraton Palace Hotel," announced Sims. "We're coming away with an agreement covering thirty-three hotels!"

The hotels had agreed to hire people of color at rates in proportion to their population and to give public records of their progress during the next two years. The agreement was signed by the Ad Hoc

Committee members and endorsed by the UFM, including the NAACP, CORE and, despite their denunciations of the protest methods, the Baptist Ministers Union.

The fallout from the agreement was felt in many circles. The *Chronicle* denounced the tactics of "avowed Marxist-Leninists" and former San Francisco Mayor Roger Lapham sharply criticized the hotels for "knuckling under to pressure." Even Governor Edmund G. Brown got into the act: "These young people, 75 percent of whom are white, according to my reports, violated the law and have little in common with the responsible Negro leadership of San Francisco."[18]

But the Black leadership of the San Francisco Civil Rights Movement would hear none of it. Nowhere to be found were criticisms from the local NAACP or CORE. Both organizations were also in the Palace Hotel struggle and had members arrested as well. The movement was gaining steam, despite large numbers of fines and court tie-ups resulting from the arrests, and—more important—winning huge job concessions from San Francisco's power structure.

Driving Auto Row Crazy

On March 11, 1964, hard on the heels of the successful campaigns against Mel's, Lucky's and the hotels, the local NAACP assumed leadership in a campaign targeting discriminatory hiring practices of car dealers on San Francisco's famed Auto Row on Van Ness Avenue. The NAACP and its allies insisted that more Blacks and other people of color be hired as workers "in the whole spectrum of jobs in the automobile industry—not just mechanics, but salesmen, clerks and accountants."[19]

On March 13, Mayor Shelley and Governor Brown convened a summit session on the issue of continued civil disobedience and its impact on corporations in San Francisco and the state. Hoping, they said, to keep civil rights disputes "in the hearing room and not in the streets," they called the high-level meeting in order to prevent "a state-wide pattern from being set." Brown stated the following day that he would not tolerate any repetition of such "unruly demonstrations" as had taken place at the Palace.[20]

Soon thereafter, there was a meeting in the Mayor's office with leading corporate leaders, including officials from the Bank of America, Wells Fargo, Macy's, Levi-Strauss, Pacific Telephone and Telegraph and the San Francisco Employers Association, among others. T'Shaka noted that the Bank of America "feared it was next on the hit list."

Meanwhile, the NAACP still had its eye on Auto Row's employment practices, and had targeted the Cadillac Agency. On March 14, 107 pickets were arrested at the Cadillac showroom and forcefully put into police paddy wagons and taken off to jail. The next day, Burbridge led about sixty demonstrators in a picket line inside the Cadillac dealership showroom, singing and chanting freedom slogans for an hour as salesmen watched.

Then on April 11, hundreds of demonstrators poured into several of the major showrooms on Auto Row, while thousands of other demonstrators lined their sidewalks. Demonstrators used new tactics, packing themselves into and lying under cars, waiting to be arrested. Dismayed Chrysler-Plymouth Manager Jack Kent attempted to talk the demonstrators out of his showroom. "We believe in equal job opportunity," the exasperated manager said, "but applicants must be properly trained and capable." Demonstrators ignored Kent and entered the offices of sales manager Joseph McGoldrick. One Black picket dropped to his knees in front of McGoldrick and mockingly said, "Please Mr. Charley, give a Black boy a job." Another Black demonstrator sat at McGoldrick's desk, saying "We don't hire no niggers here."[21]

San Francisco Police arrived and set a new San Francisco record by arresting 226 people. Four hours after the demonstrations began at noon, police had cleared the area, but not before national media attention had been turned to Auto Row.

On the afternoon of April 18, with nearly 5,000 demonstrators parading peacefully in front of seven Auto Row dealers, Burbridge announced to the crowd, "You have won a victory...we have an agreement." The dealers were forced to increase minority hiring to 15 to 20 percent of their total employees.

In the wake of the largest numbers of arrests in San Francisco's civil rights history, the San Francisco Civil Rights Movement had added another huge feather to its cap. And across the country, NAACP local affiliates in more than fifty cities, including New York and Detroit, scheduled a nationwide drive to increase Black hiring to begin on May 4.

Challenging "The Most Powerful Bank in the World"

"Within the movement, we all choose projects," said Burbridge after the NAACP celebrated its victory over the auto dealers. "The Ad Hoc Committee went after the hotels, the NAACP had the auto dealers, and CORE has the banks."[22]

As it turned out, Bank of America's fear that it was "next on the hit list" was on the money. Its officials had watched nervously as the United Freedom Movement had won major concessions from employers. They knew that being one of the city's most visible corporations meant they would soon be a target. They were right. But when CORE demanded that the bank turn over a "racial census," the bank stonewalled.

CORE was fairly confident it could win. According to CORE's regional field secretary, Genevieve Hughes, "Civil rights is so red-hot just now in the Bay Area that the white folks are scared out of their minds. We can do anything we want. Every newscast is civil rights. It may be that the day has finally come when no matter what CORE does or how it does it, it still wins."[23]

When the bank finally made its "racial census" available to the local media, it showed that out of more than 30,000 employees statewide, fewer than 600 were African Americans, less than two percent of all workers. The percentages were only slightly higher for Asians and Latinos. Even in the Bay Area, with its greater number of Blacks, there were only about 200 Blacks on the bank's payroll. A Bank of America spokesperson claimed that these figures were representative of the bank's commitment to "equal opportunity for minorities."

In negotiations, CORE demanded that the bank hire up to 3,600 people of color across the state and provide 350 to 600 additional jobs for Blacks in the Bay Area alone within six months. The bank was intransigent. It said it was not interested in dealing with a local movement whose "only mandate comes from the streets."[24]

On May 20, CORE announced that it would kick off "the biggest demonstrations anybody ever saw anywhere" against what many believed to be the most powerful bank in the world.

"We knew we couldn't conduct another shop-in," recalled

T'Shaka, "so we had to figure out how to put the pressure on them. We figured that a bank rests on the faith and confidence of the public, so the best strategy would be to hurt its image somehow."[25] The strategy, developed in CORE's regional and local offices, was for protesters to camp out every day in front of the bank's branches. They knew the spectacle of people chanting slogans and carrying signs equating the bank's hiring practices with the racism of the South would not sit well with the image-conscious bank.

On March 22, mass picketing began at bank branches in thirteen California cities—from Sacramento to San Diego. And CORE employed some new direct action tactics. Members entered the bank and went to the tellers' windows, where they requested pennies and other coins in exchange for their dollar bills. After they received their change, the protesters went to another teller and had the change converted back into bills. The effect of the "bank-in" was to create long lines for service, slowing down the regular operations of the branch.

The bank continued to resist CORE's demands, saying it and the Fair Employment Practices Commission (FEPC) would not even consider "hiring quotas." But CORE leaders maintained that its employment demands, which were increased to 800 jobs in the Bay Area for Blacks, were not quotas but "a realistic goal based upon the bank's internal structure." If the demands were not met soon, CORE explained, "then statewide CORE will remain in the streets" until they are.

In June, CORE announced that it would also picket President Lyndon B. Johnson's upcoming visit to San Francisco in order to urge the president to take more aggressive action on behalf of civil rights in the South and to intervene in the prosecutions of protesters arrested during local sit-ins. The city responded by deploying the largest police detail in its history to protect Johnson. News of CORE's plans brought sharp criticism from Mayor Shelley, who wanted to spare the city further national embarrassment, and from Governor Brown, who chastised CORE for showing "rank ingratitude" toward a president who was making a "great all out fight at political peril for the civil rights bill."[26]

CORE couldn't find much to be grateful for; the community was still reeling from layoffs and the pace of hiring agreements was beginning to slow. The bank's stubborn refusal to meet any of CORE's demands added to the frustration.

Protests continued at the Bank of America. On one occasion, nearly 10,000 people surrounded a branch in the heart of San Francisco's tourist center, next to the cable car turn-around and close to Union Square and the downtown department stores.

Finally, after three months of protest, CORE announced that its pickets would leave. "The bank has met our minimal expectations," T'Shaka announced, by hiring more than 300 Blacks in the previous thirty days alone.[27] Six weeks later, the FEPC announced that the bank had indeed increased its Black employment figures by nearly forty percent, not quite the number CORE had hoped for, but a significant increase nonetheless. Wells Fargo Bank and other major local financial institutions, sensing that they might be targeted next, also signed major hiring agreements with the FEPC.

Despite Bank of America's frequent claims to the contrary, CORE and the local movement had been instrumental in their capitulation. It is highly doubtful that the bank would have hired up to 400 new Black workers in short order, much less even a few, without a mass-organized movement demanding accountability.

The victory over "the most powerful bank in the world" was the last of the large-scale wins for the jobs movement. Its success had been bought with jailings and stiff court fines, but the benefits were hundreds of new jobs for the community.

Wresting the Power of the Pencil and Paper

The struggle for jobs in San Francisco also took its toll on local organizations. The UFM was effectively dissolved after the major demonstrations; the Baptist Ministers Union, which had distanced itself from some of the more controversial direct action tactics during the early months of 1964, had made the coalition a fragile one from the beginning. However, San Francisco CORE had become a major influence on its national body, forcing the James Farmer-led organization into a more radical view of the larger movement.

Carlton Goodlett, longtime community leader and publisher of the city's biggest African American newspaper, the *Sun-Reporter,* understood why the militant organizations in San Francisco drew the wrath of the power structure. "You have turned this town upside down," he said. "You have accomplished more than the leaders of my generation did in 15 years. They don't like you because you're changing things."[28]

Much had in fact changed. But the reality of economic discrimination, though challenged and dented, remained. Before the wave of demonstrations hit San Francisco, novelist James Baldwin toured the city in 1964 for a public television documentary and pointed out the underlying problem. "All right," Baldwin said, "they talk about the South. The South is not half as bad as San Francisco. The white man, he's not taking advantage of you in public like they're doing down in Birmingham, but he's killing you with that pencil and paper, brother. This city is a somewhat better place to lie about is really all it comes to."[27]

The San Francisco Civil Rights Movement was premised on the understanding that the real power was in "the pencil and paper" of economic and employment discrimination. Working from the grassroots, it was successful in delivering hundreds of jobs from the powerful interests who controlled the pencil and paper. For a while, anyway, the movement wrestled control from the corporations and challenged them on a scale unprecedented in the city's history.

The victories for civil rights organizations in San Francisco not only shattered the myth of a contented Black population, but also led directly to the development of a more politically active Bay Area community. A large number of the students involved in the Free Speech Movement that began at the University of California at Berkeley, for example, had cut their political teeth during the jobs struggles in San Francisco.

Many of the African American activists who had worked with CORE, the NAACP and other civil rights groups became increasingly militant as they turned their attention to other issues. Some joined the Black Panther Party, others helped wage struggles for inclusive education and ethnic studies at San Francisco State College and other schools.

The San Francisco Civil Rights Movement of the 1960s demonstrated that it is possible to act on a large scale to improve the material condition of a hurting community. It did so by refusing to be limited by what was "reasonable" or even legal, and by countering the power of large local corporations with mass collective action. The times are different, but the imperative remains the same.

NOTES

1. Marable, *Race, Reform and Rebellion,* p. 54.

2. Oba T'Shaka, interview with author, San Francisco State University, April 1993.

3. Daniels, *Pioneer Urbanites,* p. 165, quoting Charles S. Johnson, *The Negro Worker in San Francisco: A Local Self-Survey (1944),* pp.79–81.

4. Quoted in Broussard, *Black San Francisco,* p. 239.

5. Record, *Minority Groups and Intergroup Relations,* p. 13.

6. Marable, p. 54.

7. Record, p. 3.

8. Hemp, "Jim Crow-Race Barrier in Our City," *San Francisco Chronicle,* August 20, 1963.

9. See note 2.

10. Ibid.

11. "Negro Leader Threatens 'Attack on Pocketbooks,'" *San Francisco Chronicle,* August 20, 1963.

12. "Mass S.F. Sit-In Arrests—Dobbs, Shelley Argue," *San Francisco Chronicle,* November 4, 1963.

13. Ibid.

14. "Pickets Resume Drive-In Siege," *San Francisco Chronicle,* November 7, 1963.

15. "Pastors Rap CORE 'Shop-Ins,'" *San Francisco Chronicle,* February 26, 1964.

16. Graham, "Mass Arrest Of Pickets at Palace Hotel," *San Francisco Chronicle,* March 2, 1964; "Litters for Passive Pickets?" *San Francisco Examiner,* March 4, 1964. See "We Shall Overcome," *San Francisco,* 6:10, p.27.

17. "A Truce in Palace Picketing," *San Francisco Chronicle,* March 3, 1964.

18. Jackson Doyle, "Brown Hits the Sit-In at Palace." *San Francisco Chronicle,* March 11, 1964.

19. Robertson, "Sharp Warning to SF Auto Dealers," *San Franicsco Chronicle,* April 16, 1964.

20. Wax, "Summit Session on Rights—Brown, Shelley Peace Plan," *San Francisco Chronicle,* March 14, 1964.

21. Donoran, "'Auto Row' Protest—226 Sit-In Arrests," *San Francisco Chronicle,* April 12, 1964.

22. "CORE Rally in Grace Cathedral," *San Francisco Chronicle,* April 18, 1964.

23. Meier and Rudwick, *CORE,* p. 229.

24. "B of A Says CORE Acts in Bad Faith," *San Francisco Chronicle,* May 20, 1964.

25. Professor Oba T'Shaka in class, "Black Politics and Liberation Themes," San Francisco State University, Spring 1992.

26. "Massive S.F. Security for Johnson," *San Francisco Chronicle,* June 18, 1964.

27. "Rousing Rally for 'Freedom Fighters,'" *San Francisco Chronicle,* July 28, 1964.

28. Robertson, "Baldwin's TV Tour of S.F. Negroes," *San Francisco Chronicle,* February 4, 1964.

CHAPTER SIX

"Stand on a Street and Bounce a Ball"

Organizing the Mississippi Freedom Democratic Party

Very few people in 1964 thought it was possible for a grassroots movement led by poor southern Blacks to establish a new national political agenda. But the struggle for voting rights in Mississippi during the summer of '64—led by the Student Nonviolent Coordinating Committee (SNCC) and the newly created Mississippi Freedom Democratic Party (MFDP)—did exactly that. It showed just how people taking action can have an impact on an entire nation.

Mississippi's reputation as the state with the most rigid and violent racial caste system was well known throughout the country and, of course, among African Americans living in the state. Since the betrayal of Reconstruction in 1877, when the national government pulled troops out of the occupied former Confederacy following the Civil War, African Americans had been disenfranchised through the actions of white vigilante terrorism as well as through "legitimate" methods such as grandfather clauses (you could only vote if your grandfather had voted), poll taxes and literacy tests (Blacks were required to be able to "read and interpret" the state constitution before being allowed to register). Sharecropping and the crop-lien system, together with laws that only recognized white people's rights, ushered in a new slavery in the 20th century.

White supremacy not only ruled, it was enforced violently. Black comedian Dick Gregory later described a white "moderate" in the state as "a cat who wants to lynch you from a low tree."[1] In fact, lynchings were used as a form of political intimidation after the demise of Reconstruction. Between 1880 and 1940, almost 600 Blacks were lynched by whites in Mississippi alone. The pretext: Blacks were a threat to white civilization and to the innocence of women and children. The real reasons: Blacks were trying to exercise some economic and political clout by demanding their rights. Black Mississippians quickly learned the price of "agitating."

Efforts to force the issue on the right of Blacks to vote accelerated after a 1944 Supreme Court decision outlawed the "white primary." In 1946, Medgar Evers and a group of Black veterans returning from World War II went to the county courthouse in Decatur to demand the right to vote. These men, who had put their lives on the line fighting in Europe, were soon surrounded by a mob of whites with guns. But to call them a mob suggests that they were going against convention, that they were lawless. In Mississippi, white mob rule was the norm, and was encouraged even in the highest state offices. Theodore Bilbo, a U.S. Senator from the state, worried that "if you let a handful [of Blacks] go to the polls...there will be two handfuls [later]." His solution: "You and I know what's the best way to keep the niggers from voting. You do it the night before the election. I don't have to tell you any more than that. Red-blooded men know what I mean." Even the *Jackson Daily News* offered front-page advice to Blacks thinking of going to the polls in the late 1940s: "DON'T TRY IT!"[2]

Since the days of slavery, Blacks in Mississippi had been the poorest and the least educated group in the state. In the 1950s, median Black family income was about $600 a year. About three of every four African Americans over the age of 25 had less than a seventh-grade education, and only about two percent ever graduated from high school. Despite a large out-migration, nearly half of the state's population was Black—the highest rate of any state—yet only about five percent were registered to vote and only two percent actually voted.

Because Blacks constituted a majority in most counties, they could have controlled most of the state's political agenda through the ballot box. But as the federal courts established greater avenues for voter participation, Mississippi erected more barriers to participation by Blacks. Though the Fourteenth Amendment to the Constitution, passed after the Civil War, guaranteed Black males the right to vote, poll taxes and literacy tests in many southern states effectively prevented them from doing so. At the end of the 1950s, Mississippi placed new requirements on those wanting to register to vote, though the hurdles were mostly imposed on Blacks who went to the county courthouse to register. They were asked to copy a section of the state constitution, read it and give a "reasonable interpretation." Then they were asked to write a statement "setting forth your understanding of the duties and obligations of citizenship under a constitutional form of government." Even one of the legislators who helped draft the new guidelines admitted that "if I wasn't already registered, I don't believe I could qualify myself."[3]

Because Blacks were thus cut off from opportunities to use their potential electoral power to achieve needed economic gains, many organizers saw the vote as the single most important issue to be addressed. But those who advocated for the right to vote had to do so quietly. In the climate of the times, belonging to the National Association for the Advancement of Colored People (NAACP) could mean a lynching. Most whites regarded the NAACP as a Communist organization bent on destroying everything that the heroes of the Confederacy had fought to preserve. Before the 1950s, only about 120 members of the country's largest civil rights group could be found in the entire state.

By the late 1950s and early 1960s, the Civil Rights Movement had spread to many places throughout the South and in other parts of the country. But Mississippi was different. It was said that trying to organize for civil rights in Mississippi was "like trying to pick a plantation's entire cotton crop single-handedly—one boll at a time, in the middle of the night, with a gun pointed at your head."[4] Civil rights organizations had encountered great difficulties in other campaigns in other places, but most had considered Mississippi, circa 1964, far too dangerous.

Little by little, however, in county after county, NAACP branches were established in the state. Aaron Henry helped organize a chapter in Clarksdale; Amzie Moore in Cleveland; Clinton Battle in Indianola; in Pike County, Curtis Conway (C.C.) Bryant was elected branch chapter president, and in the Ku Klux Klan stronghold of Amite County, E.W. Steptoe helped put together another office.[6] It has to be remembered—especially for those who dismiss the civil rights work of this generation as "reformist" or "integrationist" or even "irrelevant for today's times"—that organizing an NAACP chapter was as militant as you could be at the time. It could get you killed.

In fact, the killings of Medgar Evers, Louis Allen and Herbert Lee, to name but a few of the NAACP's early martyrs, demonstrated quite clearly that one could expect to pay the ultimate price for being courageous enough to organize for basic human rights. Soon, though, the NAACP would be joined by the young organizers from the Student Nonviolent Coordinating Committee, or SNCC (pronounced "snick").

Organized in 1960, SNCC's direct-action techniques, such as the sit-in campaigns in which Black protesters refused to move from "white-only" counters until they were served, made them a force to be reckoned with. The SNCC organizers and their campaign spread to many cities across the country. One of their young leaders, Bob Moses, had begun making contacts in Mississippi with, among others, Amzie Moore, C.C. Bryant and Webb Owens of the NAACP. Intrigued by the possibility of conducting a voter registration campaign, Moses pushed for greater SNCC commitment in the Mississippi town of McComb. In 1961, SNCC workers began going door-to-door in attempts to educate McComb's Black residents about their voting rights.

Resistance to Registration

Still small in number, though, SNCC's staff could not withstand the tremendous resistance of the local whites, who arrested them and otherwise used violent intimidation to deter them. The project faltered and SNCC organizers moved onto other campaigns, but did not forget about Mississippi. The next year, SNCC received funding from the Voter Education Project to conduct a registration campaign, allowing their field workers "to live with the people [of Mississippi], develop their own leaders and teach them the process of registration and effective use of the franchise." Moses arranged for some of the young activists to receive training at the well-respected Highlander Folk School in Tennessee, since training (or "agitating") in Mississippi was deemed too dangerous.

By this time, SNCC had made what would be the pivotal decision in relation to organizing in Mississippi, a decision that, according to some observers, led to the emergence of a sustained movement in the South. SNCC made the commitment to create a "cadre of locally based, full-time grassroots organizers" who could give the Amzie Moores and the C.C. Bryants the day-to-day assistance they needed to organize their communities.

Charles Payne's *I've Got the Light of Freedom,* an excellent book on organizing in Mississippi, documents the "slow and respectful work" that was the backbone of the movement. Without the canvassing, the phone calls, the mass meetings, the countless follow-ups, there would have been no SNCC and no Mississippi Freedom Democratic Party (MFDP). In short, there would have been no movement. Unfortunately, this slow, daily building of the civil rights struggle is too often muted when placed next to the personalities and the famous events and oratory of the era. SNCC organizer Marshall Ganz put it simply enough:

> Marches help to remove some of the external barriers to the Negro people's freedom. They do little to emancipate people from within...It is by talking and acting together—on their own initiative and their own decision—that some of these bonds begin to be loosed.[5]

Bob Moses later talked about how SNCC workers tried to build relationships. The way to organize a town, he said, is "by bouncing a ball. You stand on a street and bounce a ball. Soon all the children come around. You keep on bouncing the ball. Before long, it runs under someone's porch and then you meet the adults."[6]

In this simple way, Moses described SNCC's philosophy of building a movement. In order for the movement to make a lasting impact on people's lives, it had to involve them in the planning and execution of strategy. People had to see that they had a stake in the movement and that they were more valuable than simply as warm bodies in a demonstration.

Payne writes that organizers had to be a little of everything, including "morale boosters, teachers, welfare agents, transportation coordinators, canvassers, public speakers, negotiators, lawyers, all while communicating with people ranging from illiterate sharecroppers to well-off professionals...Exciting days and major victories are rare. Progress is a few dollars raised, a few more people coming to pay a poll tax."[7]

Local people learned to trust SNCC organizers because the SNCC people had done their homework, and had built relationships with respected people in the community. Community people admired the young organizers' tenacity and courage and to this day speak fondly of them.

A Vote for Freedom

Late in 1962, several civil rights groups—the NAACP, the Southern Christian Leadership Conference (SCLC) and the Congress of Racial Equality—joined SNCC in a new umbrella group called the Council of Federated Organizations (COFO). Basically controlled and run by SNCC, COFO's first project was to conduct a mock election in the fall of 1963 in which unofficial "Freedom Party" candidates would challenge the state's entrenched white Democratic candidates.

The project was termed "Freedom Vote." But in order to achieve participation from Mississippi Blacks, the project would need more volunteers. White students from northern universities like Yale and Stanford were also brought in to help get out the Freedom Vote and, despite intensified brutality from local whites, the campaign carried on. SNCC began to train local residents in the dozens of Mississippi towns where the vote would be held.

Most of these residents, many of whom worked in the fields as sharecroppers, had never been involved in community organizing. One of them was Fannie Lou Hamer. Hamer was to become a legend in the movement as a result of her role in getting the SNCC project off the ground. Her courage and honest commitment to the work inspired hundreds of Black Mississippians to involve themselves in the movement.

SNCC's philosophy of training local people to work on various campaigns and eventually become leaders and maintain independent organizations was in sharp contrast to the practice of other large civil rights organizations, who felt it was wisest to have national leaders make the pivotal and directional decisions in local campaigns. "Our adherence to the organizing principle that you find people who are already working and build on what they are doing was the basis of our strength," SNCC's Jean Wheeler Smith later said.[8]

The mock election was a wild success, with 83,000 people casting their "votes" at barbershops, beauty parlors and sidewalk tables in places like Jackson, Lawndale, Philadelphia, Meridian, Clinton and McComb. The Freedom Party candidates won easily over the regular white Democratic candidates, proving that, despite segregationist claims to the contrary, Blacks were indeed interested in casting ballots to determine their futures. The result of the Freedom Vote campaign also served SNCC's longer range goals in that it provided practice in voting to people who had never done so in their lives.

The success of the Freedom Vote led COFO to approve Moses' plan for a more ambitious project the following summer that came to be known as the Mississippi Summer Project, with voter registration as its cornerstone. Originally the plan was to use the current COFO workers with more, mostly white, students from northern schools to register as many Black voters as possible so they could cast real ballots in the upcoming elections.

Yet it became clear to staff at a SNCC meeting in April 1964 that as long as the official state Democratic and Republican parties were effectively closed to African Americans and their needs, it would be pointless to simply register people for the sake of it. The question repeated over and over at SNCC strategy meetings was: What good will it do to vote if there isn't anybody or anything to vote for? An independent political party—one that would address the concerns of Black and all poor Mississippians and attempt to change the relations of power in the state's political system—became the talk of SNCC.

Delegates from the Grassroots

Suddenly the project known as "Freedom Summer" took on new dimensions. SNCC established the Mississippi Freedom Democratic Party (MFDP) in order to help along voter registration, show the strength of Black voter participation and challenge and eventually succeed the state's whites-only Democratic party. SNCC field secretary and native Mississippian Lawrence Guyot was named chairman, and longtime Southern Christian Leadership Conference (SCLC) activist Ella Baker, who had been active in founding and building SNCC in 1960, gave the keynote address at the founding convention.

Those attending the MFDP convention were not typical party delegates. Of the forty-seven MFDP delegates representing Leflore County, for example, (one of the five congressional districts in the state), almost one-third came from rural communities or plantations. Some had been teachers at SNCC's Freedom Schools, including Mary Diggs, Alice Blackwell, Laura McGhee, Ethel Brady and Pinkie Pilcher. The resolutions that first county convention passed reflected both movement issues (federal protection for civil rights workers and better housing) as well as traditional bread-and-butter political issues (better street lighting, more school crossing guards and garbage disposal).

More than 1,000 people working on the organizing project throughout the state were arrested and countless more harassed during the summer. James Chaney, a Black Mississippi native, and northern volunteers Michael Schwerner and Andrew Goodman were killed outside of Philadelphia (Miss.). In Hattiesburg, the homes of MFDP leaders were bombed, and in Holly Springs the local police surrounded a schoolhouse where an MFDP precinct meeting was being held.

Still, compared with the intimidating nature of regular voter registration at the courthouse, MFDP registration could be done entirely within Black communities—in churches, local stores, homes—and it could be accomplished with the use of a simple registration form. The work SNCC organizers had done to train local people as organizers paid off in a big way during the registration campaign. For example, Mrs. Susie Morgan and Mrs. Lula Belle Johnson, two MFDP canvassers, would go into people's homes and say, "You know I'm Black and poor, just like you are. You know I wouldn't tell you nothing wrong."[9]

Mass meetings, a key part in the organizing drive, helped keep spirits strong. Charles Payne writes that meetings in which someone like Fannie Lou Hamer would share testimony or a field secretary or other organizer would bring news from two counties over provided a sense of unified and purposeful community. "Meetings broke down the debilitating sense of isolation by bringing local people out so they could see that growing numbers of their neighbors were with them."[13]

By the end of August, more than 80,000 Blacks had joined the MFDP.

Challenging the Democrats

The summer registration drive and political education around the MFDP were leading to the prime target: challenging the state Democratic party at the August Democratic National Convention in Atlantic City, where the party was to nominate Lyndon B. Johnson as its presidential candidate. Despite the success of the Freedom Vote, the seemingly overnight registration of thousands of new members, and President Johnson's frequent pledges in support of civil rights legislation, the MFDP faced an uphill battle on the way to Atlantic City.

First, in order to avoid losing political support, Johnson had promised to back the regular segregationist Democratic delegates from the state. Meanwhile, the leaders of the state's Democratic party adopted a platform opposing civil rights, making it clear that they rejected Johnson and the national party's stance on this issue. This put Johnson in a difficult position, since delegates from five other Deep South states threatened to walk out of the convention if the Mississippi delegates were replaced by the upstart MFDP activists. Despite the fact that the MFDP was gaining support from delegates from other states, Johnson instructed his eventual running mate, Hubert Humphrey, to defuse the MFDP challenge quietly before the convention began.

It was in this political atmosphere that, just a couple of weeks before the start of the convention, the bodies of civil rights workers Chaney, Schwerner and Goodman were discovered at the bottom of an earthen dam near the small town of Philadelphia. The national media rushed into the state and the news coverage of the murders gave further exposure to the organizing efforts of the summer.

As a result, the MFDP state convention in Jackson was even larger than expected—nearly 3,000 delegates attended. The media portrayed the event as presaging a battle for the soul of the national party. The MFDP delegation, financed with almost all of SNCC's resources, had selected a delegation of sixty-four African Americans and four whites to lead the organization in Atlantic City. Its leaders were Hamer, Aaron Henry, Victoria Gray, Ed King and Annie Devine. Meanwhile the all-white Mississippi Democrats passed legislation banning the new party in the state, charging it was a "communist organization" bent on conspiracy. Chairman Guyot was arrested and jailed for two months on a charge dating back to a January demonstration.

Despite the arrests and jailings, there was a sense of optimism among the MFDP delegates. As one said on the eve of the convention, "Whether we're seated or not, we'll be there to tell the world that we are dissatisfied with what is happening in Mississippi." The delegates would be able to testify before the Credentials Committee, hoping to sway enough of them to seat the MFDP delegates and not the all-white delegation.

The highlight of the testimony came from Hamer, who spoke of her life as a sharecropper in Mississippi and how she decided to begin working to change the conditions of poor people in her state. She spoke of her association with SNCC and the MFDP and the harassment and beatings she had received from the police as a result. She spoke eloquently of one severe beating in particular, and concluded, "All of this on account we want to register, to become first-class citizens, and if the Freedom Democratic Party is not seated now, I question America. Is this America? The land of the free and the home of the brave? Where we have to sleep with our telephones off the hook because our lives be threatened daily?"[11]

A Moral Force for Justice

Hamer's electrifying speech was covered live on national television and it was clear that the MFDP had succeeded in placing their position as a challenge of moral force. Johnson's aides managed to interrupt network coverage of Hamer's testimony with a hastily called presidential speech discussing everything but civil rights and the MFDP challenge.

Eventually Humphrey, and his protégé Walter Mondale, offered a compromise: the MFDP could have two at-large seats at the convention and a promise that in the future no segregated party or delegation would be seated at a Democratic convention. The MFDP was furious. "We didn't come all this way for no two seats," Hamer said. But Johnson's forces had put intense pressure on MFDP's supporters inside the convention and it soon became apparent that the Mississippi activists were out of allies. Even other civil rights organizations suggested that the MFDP accept the compromise. The MFDP rejected the plan but it was clear they could not win. Bob Moses announced that he would "have nothing to do with the political system any longer." Victoria Gray said that "those unable to understand why we were not accepting the compromise didn't realize we would be betraying those very many people back there in Mississippi whom we represented."[12]

On the Tuesday night of the convention, Hamer led the MFDP contingent onto the floor and, in front of rolling cameras, took the seats reserved for the white Democrats, who had boycotted in protest of the compromise. Security guards soon arrived to remove them. By the following night the chairs had been removed, but Hamer and the delegates took to the convention floor again and denounced the party for its treatment of poor Mississippians. She then led the delegation in emotional renditions of freedom songs such as "This Little Light of Mine," and "Go Tell It on the Mountain." The scene dominated the convention (though in his presidential memoirs, Johnson summed up the convention as "a place of happy, surging crowds and thunderous cheers"). new form of resistance?

Many of those who had gone to Atlantic City in 1964 with the hopes of changing the system by using the system now realized that the liberal wing of the Democratic party, despite platitudes in support of civil rights, could not be counted on. "Never again," said SNCC's Cleveland Sellers, "would we be lulled into believing that our task was exposing injustices so that the 'good' people of America could eliminate them."[13]

From Politics to Organizing

The MFDP and SNCC scored some important gains in Atlantic City. On an organizational level, the work performed that summer brought into political activity many progressive Blacks who went on to become accomplished leaders and community organizers in other projects. The legacy of the Herbert Lees and the early NAACP folks, the young organizers with SNCC, the Fannie Lou Hamers and the everyday people in the small towns who decided to stand up and fight is that their actions opened the nation's eyes to continuing fundamental discrimination in the South. It helped set the stage for the dismantling of Jim Crow, while at the same time raising the national stakes over civil rights.

The people who did the work of that summer showed how strong the movement could be. Black people who had never voted before not only participated in the process but took on some of the most powerful people in the nation. It is, to say the least, a remarkable example of how organizing, slowly and with determination and courage, can yield impressive results.

NOTES

1. Payne, *I've Got The Light of Freedom*, p. 340.
2. Dittmer, *Local People*, pp. 1–2.
3. Ibid, p. 71.
4. Williams, *Eyes on the Prize*, p. 208.
5. Payne, p. 236.
6. Ibid, p. 243.
7. Ibid, p. 246.
8. Ibid, p. 132.
9. Ibid, p. 232.
10. Ibid, p. 259.
11. Carson, *In Struggle*, p. 126. See also Williams, *Eyes on the Prize*, p. 241.
12. Williams, pp. 242–244.
13. See Carson, pp. 122–129.

CHAPTER SEVEN
Unafraid and Dignified

Welfare Recipients Organize for Their Rights

In 1992, presidential candidate Bill Clinton promised to "end welfare as we know it." Four years later, a reelected President Clinton and a happy Republican Congress passed legislation that indeed dismantled the welfare system, sharply curtailing benefits and returning much decision-making to the states. As the barely adequate living standards of the "poorest of the poor" come under attack in state after state, where are the social justice movements?

The term "welfare reform" has had many different meanings over the past thirty years. For many, it has meant ending a "welfare state" by getting those who "won't work" off the public dole. For others, including welfare recipients and their allies who organized in the welfare rights movement that began in the 1960s, reform had an entirely different meaning. We would do well to recall what "welfare reform" meant to those receiving public assistance 30 years ago.

Prior to the 1960s, most political theory held that it was impossible to organize among the poorest of society. Poor people were considered unmotivated, content to live in their "culture of poverty." For those on welfare, feelings of unworthiness and powerlessness were common. But the organizing done by welfare recipients themselves during the 1960s and 1970s helped, at least for a while, change those perceptions.

The welfare rights movement was basically a movement of poor people for poor people. Contrary to the myths and stereotypes about the "apathy" and "laziness" of those on welfare, during the welfare rights movement large numbers of women fought for some degree of economic independence by campaigning for decent jobs and child care along with increased welfare grants.

"There are a lot of lies that male society tells about welfare mothers," former welfare recipient and welfare rights organizer Johnnie Tillmon said in 1972. "It says that AFDC mothers are immoral, that AFDC mothers are lazy, misuse their welfare checks, spend it all on booze and are stupid and incompetent. If people are willing to believe these lies, it's partly because they are just special versions of the lies that society tells about all women."[2]

Political organizers focusing on the needs of poor people originally intended to address wider economic justice issues, but it soon became apparent that the heart of the problem rested in the insufficient income provided to women with dependent children. In this context, most of the organizing work that began in the mid-1960s and continued for almost a decade centered primarily on the welfare apparatus.

Grassroots organizations focused their work on the goal of making the welfare bureaucracy accountable to the millions of poor families to whom the system routinely denied adequate income. The main purposes of welfare rights organizing were to secure benefits for recipients, to create a national organization to meet the needs of mostly welfare mothers and, eventually, to replace "the welfare" with a guaranteed income program for all Americans.

Though it would be politically unpopular today, for many welfare recipients in the 1960s, for whom a job was unattainable and unrealistic, the goal was simply to get more money. While the welfare rights movement also demanded decent-paying jobs and subsidized child care to make work truly practical, their insistence that the government provide more income seemed the more realizable demand and therefore dominated their activities. One of the most popular slogans of the movement was "Bread or Justice." For those who had neither, that seemed like a good place to start.

Fight, Don't Starve!

The welfare system in the United States was born out of a history of popular unrest. Several movements during the Depression of the 1930s were organized around poor people's concerns. World War I veterans, known as the "Bonus Marchers" because they demanded the government pay them promised extra benefits, had marched on Herbert Hoover's administration in 1932 during the Depression. Hoover said that "at least people weren't starving," and ordered the U.S. Army to drive them out of the capital. The Communist Party was especially instrumental in organizing the Workers Alliance and Unemployed Councils, which made big waves by, among other things, physically preventing evictions in their "Fight, Don't Starve" campaigns and demanding public works jobs for the millions out of work.[2]

These and many other demands were pressed by millions of people left homeless and without work in the Depression. Fearing that hungry people would create massive disruption, the new president, Franklin Roosevelt, moved quickly to put some reforms into place. The New Deal created measures to put people to work, launching the Federal Emergency and Relief Agency and passing the Social Security Act of 1935, ushering in welfare in America.

But the new "welfare state" still left countless people out in the cold. Black people complained that they were kept out of works programs and people of all backgrounds never saw the expanded pie on their tables. Before the 1960s, millions of families who were eligible for benefits didn't see a penny. Furthermore, the welfare statutes were designed to make sure there would always be an available low-wage work force, so able-bodied adults without children and two-parent families were ineligible for any relief at all.

By the 1960s, the mechanization of agriculture, especially of cotton, sent farm laborers and their families to look for better lives in the cities of the North and the West. At the same time people were migrating to urban jobs, however, the jobs were migrating out of the cities—many overseas, many more out to the exclusively white and semi-affluent suburbs. Suddenly, it seemed, the great numbers of people crowded into the cities were left with few options. Racism exacerbated these problems, as African Americans and Latinos in particular found themselves discriminated against, isolated and without means of income. Under these stresses, and because in many states only single women with children could receive welfare, divorce and desertion rates escalated dramatically, and thousands upon thousands of women were dealt a hand few anticipated and none wanted.

Even so, the number of people on welfare did not expand dramatically. Most people still viewed welfare as an option of last resort—simply put, most people did the best they could to cope. Besides, average welfare payments for a family of four in 1966 ranged from only $32 a month in Mississippi (the lowest-paying state) to an average of $146 a month nationwide. This was far less than the $270 per month designated as the official poverty line.

Moreover, applying for welfare was no walk in the park. On average, out of every three people who were eligible and applied for benefits, two were turned down. Since most recipients didn't know that the law guaranteed entitlement based on need, they rarely challenged the decisions. "The social worker made me feel like I had committed murder when I first asked for help," remembers Roxanne Jones of Philadelphia.[3]

The Next Battle Ground

The mood of the 1960s was a little different; the civil rights movement had changed the passivity of many in communities across America and people began to see that they needn't simply shut up and accept injustice—the system that kept them poor owed them more than that. Many organizers saw the crowded inner cities as the next battle ground.

"Welfare rights, in the largest sense, was really the logical next step to the Civil Rights Movement," recalled Tim Sampson, an early welfare rights organizer and today a Professor of Social Work at San Francisco State University. "The question before us was how to move the struggle into the north and deliver economic benefits to those who really needed them."[4]

The beginnings of welfare rights organizing in the 1960s cannot be found in a single place. Between 1963 and 1966, different groups came to life, all attempting to protect themselves from the injustices of a system that denied them benefits and stigmatized them for trying to provide an adequate living for their families. Groups like Aid to Needy Children (ANC) Mothers Anonymous in Los Angeles, the Committee of Needy Families on the Lower East Side in New York City and others in Ohio, Chicago, Cleveland, Boston, Baltimore and Oakland were formed independently by the people who knew best what the system presented—the recipients themselves, poor white women and poor women of color.

Said Johnnie Tillmon, then president of ANC Mothers Anonymous:

People just started talking. We found out that all over the country the attitudes of the general public and the welfare department were the same toward anybody on welfare. The people from New York got treated by the social workers and the other people the same as they did in Mississippi. In the past, most of us had been so ashamed that we were on welfare that we wouldn't even admit it to another welfare recipient. But as we talked to each other, we forgot about all that shame, and as we listened to the horrible treatment and conditions all over the country, we could begin thinking about the idea that maybe it wasn't us that should be ashamed.[5]

For organizers, it was fertile ground. Even so, after fighting a Jim Crow-style caste system and the denial of the vote, organizers had not anticipated narrowing their focus specifically to welfare rights. As one organizer put it, "the welfare recipient groups just grew so quickly that they soon took up everybody's time."[6]

Welfare was clearly an issue to organize around, and different strategies emerged as to how to connect the push for more benefits to bigger goals for economic justice. The idea of flooding the welfare rolls with recipients can be credited to two social scientists, Frances Fox Piven and Richard Cloward, who theorized that if poor people, welfare recipients in particular, could be organized to demand their rightful benefits, local budgets would collapse, the system would overload, and bureaucracies would be forced to turn to the federal government to institute a guaranteed annual income.[7]

The two academics shopped their ideas around to community organizers, eventually catching the ear of George Wiley, who by 1966 had resigned from the Congress of Racial Equality and set up the Poverty/Rights Action Center. A veteran of the civil rights movement, Wiley was looking for a way to transform the movement into a fight for economic justice. The Piven and Cloward strategy intrigued him, but ultimately he and other organizers decided to organize clients into longer-term community organizations. The rationale was simple enough: recipients should exercise more control over their destinies instead of hoping the government would eventually respond on its own.

What War on Poverty?

By 1966, President Lyndon Johnson's "War on Poverty" was little more than a public relations campaign that was enjoying generally positive media coverage. One of Johnson's "generals," Sargent Shriver of the Office of Economic Opportunity, would deliver upbeat success stories about how well the effort to end poverty in the U.S. was going. The reality was different, of course, if you were on welfare. Soon enough, the PR campaign would meet the welfare rights movement.

Early in 1966, at a news conference in Washington D.C., Shriver found himself being shouted down by about 60 welfare recipients representing small welfare rights organizations. "Tell us where the poor are being helped!" the women demanded. His weak responses were answered by shouts of "He's lying!" and "Stop listening to him." The women forced Shriver to leave the building, but staying behind was a very impressed Wiley, who recognized in these women a potential for grassroots leadership on a larger scale. Women like these were to become leaders in the new movement ("The Founding Mothers," Wiley called them), all of whom were recipients, including Etta Horn, Dovie Coleman, Carmen Olivio, Dorothy Dimascio, Edith Doering, Kate Emmerson, Marian Kidd, Bertha Hernandez, Margaret McCarthy, Alice Nixon, Frankie Jeter and Ruby Duncan.

Wiley took particular interest in Johnnie Tillmon, an African American mother of six from Los Angeles' Watts district. "The poverty program is a laugh," Tillmon bitterly remarked. "When all the money is spent, the rich will get richer and I will still be receiving a welfare check."[8]

By the summer of 1966, some of the disconnected welfare rights activity around the country was being coordinated. Like the Watts group, most of the small groups from around the country had been formed to push for more benefits and to support other women on welfare. In Ohio, welfare recipient Edith Doering and the Reverend Paul Younger helped organize welfare mothers and other poor people into a 150-mile walk from Cleveland to Columbus, the capital. Taunted with racial epithets and shouts of "Why don't you get jobs?" the 100 or so marchers began walking on June 20, singing:

> We feed our children bread and beans
> While rich folks ride in limousines.
> After all we're human beings,
> Marching down Columbus Road.[9]

When they finally reached the capital, their number had grown to 2,000. In twenty-five other cities—Philadelphia, Baltimore, Louisville, Chicago, San Bernardino (Calif.), New York and Boston among them—similar demonstrations converged on government offices and agencies.

On June 30, 1966, the day known as "the birth of a movement," more than 100 different groups demanding adequate income held large demonstrations across the county. In Louisville, more than a hundred people, led by Hulbert James, demanded that the food stamp program be available for poor people in Jefferson County; in Philadelphia, a couple of hundred men, women and their children conducted a "sleep-out" at a government building demanding AFDC payment increases; in Boston, mothers demanded the right to supplement welfare checks with earnings and asked the state to stop using the condescending term "illegitimate" to describe some of their children.

Wiley's Poverty/Rights Action Center had been instrumental in coordinating the national protests. It became clear right away that something new was on the horizon. Poor people were moving and there was excitement in the air. The different welfare rights groups that emerged eventually came together in 1967 to form the National Welfare Rights Organization (NWRO). With its founding came an increase in organizing (at its peak, NWRO had more than 120,000 members—including the children of recipient families) and more bold direct action campaigns.

The NWRO set out to bring four fundamental rights into a welfare system most recipients considered inhumane, cold and discriminatory: adequate income, dignity, justice and democracy. The NWRO adopted a thirteen-point Welfare Bill of Rights, including the right to be a member of a welfare rights organization, the right to equal treatment regardless of race, the right to appeal a decision made by local welfare departments and the right to privacy.

Though NWRO represented a national movement, welfare rights activity was not based on a centralized decision-making process. Many of the strategies and organizing drives were similar, but local communities had different experiences, both successes and failures. Nevertheless, most groups saw the benefits of belonging to a larger national "movement," and their members paid dues to NWRO. NWRO asked for only a dollar a year from its membership and in its constitution required that affiliated groups have at least 25 members (there were more than 500 welfare rights groups nationally, of which about 400 met the 25-member requirement) and that a majority of each group must be welfare recipients. All but 10 percent of members were low-income people. Still, each local group was independent of NWRO and therefore could exercise its own decision-making as its members saw fit.

A Movement for All Poor People

NWRO was explicitly committed to organizing across racial lines, with only a person's poverty to qualify them. This was in contrast to the calls for "Black Power" and nationalist rhetoric of the late 1960s that called for building power bases according to race.

The NWRO movement to help all poor people would be a uniting factor amidst all the harsh debate about who was most oppressed. After all, the majority of the poor in the U.S. were white, with millions more coming out of Puerto Rican, Mexican American, Native American and other communities. As Mrs. Lilia Calloway, a Black welfare recipient and mother from D.C. said, "This [movement] is for all the people, not just Negroes."[10]

Poor white women didn't have to be convinced that the Black welfare mother was a stereotype. Countless white women also faced daily struggles with their local welfare bureaucracies. Shirley Dalton, a white woman from West Virginia, talked about her experience trying to provide for her family. "I went to Morgantown and asked for welfare for coal. They wouldn't give it to me. They gave me a seven-dollar food stamp for the nine of us. Now that's what we lived off for a month. I had one loaf of bread to divide between us."[11] Still, though white women made up between 10 and 20 percent of those who participated in welfare rights organizing, many more remained uninvolved, regarding NWRO as a militant Black movement.

The welfare rights movement raised some uncomfortable issues with the ongoing Civil Rights Movement. While welfare rights activity did emerge in rural areas of the South and Appalachia, most of the organizing, in fact most of the direct need, was in the inner cities of the North. In the mid-1960s, the Southern-based Civil Rights Movement tried to turn its work to Northern cities, but largely floundered because of its inexperience with the economic realities of the ghettos and barrios.

Though it seemed that the basis for civil rights activity working for racial justice in the North and the increasing demand (by mostly Black women) for "economic justice" were the same, many old-guard civil rights organizations, like the moderate NAACP, the Urban League, and even radicalized groups like SNCC, disavowed or refused to lend much support to the WROs emerging across the country. With a few exceptions, including the SCLC, some Black Panther Party chapters and a couple of CORE affiliates in New York and Detroit, most work being done on "civil rights" in the North ignored the issue of welfare.

"To a lot of people in the civil rights movement, they just wanted to make Black America more respectable to white America," said Deborah Amos, a welfare recipient who was involved with the Alameda County (Calif.) Welfare Rights Organization. "The idea was that look, we're no different from you, allow us into the mainstream and we'll be good citizens. So then when a lot of folks who were trying to get a few jobs for some college educated people or a place at the lunch counter saw these poor, Black women demanding welfare, of all things, they were a little embarrassed. I think they wanted to keep us hidden away in the closet."[12]

Alongside prolonged and noisy protests against the war in Vietnam, racial tension grew and inner-city rioting became more frequent in the mid-to-late-1960s. The federal government looked to expand some services and create some opportunities for poor people before these "disturbances" became everyday occurrences.

Through its Office of Economic Opportunity (OEO), local organizing was often directly subsidized by Uncle Sam. Groups like Mobilization for Youth in New York's Lower East Side formed as part of the federally funded Community Action Program and many storefront groups were able to take advantage of VISTA workers (Volunteers in Service to America, a kind of domestic Peace Corps) as a result of OEO dollars.

Brooklyn Mothers Take Action

In New York City, the largest and most influential of the poor people's organizations was the Brooklyn Welfare Action Council (B-WAC). Established by middle-aged women of color, most of whom were welfare recipients, by 1968 B-WAC could claim about 40 percent of the national membership of NWRO.

In New York City, about half of all applicants were denied aid while many more were kept off the rolls until they depleted their own meager resources. Those who were able to get some aid still had to endure repeated visits to the welfare centers, with their long waits, lack of child care and often patronizing workers. Former recipient Jackie Pope described a typical welfare office:

> Walls were dirty green or beige; desks and chairs were old and needed repair. The unspeakably repulsive toilets often flooded and there were almost never any tissues. Personnel facilities were only slightly better. With little or no privacy, staff (mostly young white men and women) sat hunched over their desks trying to confer with clients...and asserted their authority in ways so disrespectful to recipients that it generated an atmosphere of mutual dislike and distrust.[13]

Across the country, local welfare bureaucracies worked to keep the public assistance rolls small. One administrator admitted, "We tell people we are going to help them. Yet we don't pay them enough to met their needs, we penalize them for trying to keep their families together. The entire system is designed to...keep them in their place."[14]

Another former recipient, and later NWRO leader, Beulah Sanders, told Congress that the welfare bureaucracy has "made welfare clients for the past thirty years feel that, you know, they are dirt and they have no voice at all...The welfare recipients are tired. They are tired of people dictating to them telling them how they must live."[15]

Before B-WAC and NWRO came onto the scene, most aid recipients—and in fact many officials on the local level—were unaware of the full entitlement amounts recipients were due. Once organizations like B-WAC researched and disseminated information in "Know Your Welfare Rights" pamphlets, members began to demand higher monthly benefits.

B-WAC also instituted training sessions for recipients who were going into the field to recruit new members. Trainings included everything from classes on welfare rules and legal rights to organizing skills (doorknocking and other "approach" methods) and political education about who ran what in their communities. Caseworkers began to complain to their bosses that the recipients knew more about the welfare department's structure than they did.

New York's welfare grants were, on average, 15 percent below the poverty line. Further, B-WAC discovered that New York State law authorized additional money for "special needs" such as furniture, winter clothing, washing machines, paint, and air conditioners for asthmatics and other people with lung problems to bring people's living conditions up to what was called "minimum standards."

B-WAC organizers not only got some of these special allotments, they used them as an organizing tactic. Hoping to recruit new members as well as show "the department" the potential for pressure from the bottom, organizers like Joyce Burson, Andrea Kydd and Rhoda Linton, along with new members who were mostly Black and Puerto Rican women and their children, showed up at welfare centers displaying newly cut checks and loudly telling people in line what they were eligible for. Often, every client in the center would join B-WAC on the spot. Panicked, department officials released as many checks and grant vouchers as was necessary to clear the premises. B-WAC members also set up tables outside welfare offices to inform incoming recipients of their new "welfare rights."[16] One welfare official, surprised at a demonstration outside his office, remarked that he hadn't seen such a thing since the Depression.[17]

The *New York Times* reported on "bands of organized clients... demanding special grants. The demonstrators have jammed the centers, sometimes camping out in them overnight, broken down administrative procedure, played havoc with the mountains of paperwork and have been increasingly successful." Welfare organizing, the *Times* concluded, had "thrown the city's welfare program into a state of crisis and chaos."[18]

Through direct action protests like these, the New York City movement was able to secure the release of millions of dollars in AFDC grants, which increased from just over $30 million in total grants in 1963 to more than $150 million by 1968, a 500 percent increase.

Across the country, the welfare movement was employing similarly bold direct action techniques and getting a good deal of publicity for them—along with attention from the FBI and other police agencies. NWRO leader Hulbert James said in 1969 that "if there were not a Black Panther movement in this country right now, it would be the National Welfare Rights Organization that would be hauled off to jail."[19]

Groups around the country were pressing for other needs to be met as well. Phone services at discounted rates, bank accounts and credit in major department stores were all concerns high on the list of recipient demands. People on welfare often complained that the only credit they could get was from loan sharks or small neighborhood businesses that charged exorbitant interest rates.

B-WAC's last major campaign targeted Korvette's, a department store frequented by welfare clients. B-WAC members would go into stores on designated days and bring up to the cash register hundreds of dollars' worth of goods. When asked for payment, they would break out their welfare cards and say, "Charge it to the Welfare Department." Long lines and general disruption resulted and other customers became angry. B-WAC's actions inspired similar demonstrations at stores around the country, especially Sears. Finally, Sears, Gimbels, Korvettes and other stores extended credit lines to recipients on demand.

Community folks who were active in fighting for welfare benefits and economic improvement also made the connections to other issues. In St. Louis, for example, Jean King and Ivory Perry, whose first community organizing efforts were to help form the local

NWRO, protested the fact that St. Louis families on AFDC received a maximum of just over $1,400 annually, when the government's poverty line stood at $5,550.

Perry remarked on the system within which welfare recipients had to struggle:

> If they had employment for everyone, they wouldn't need to have no welfare. The way society's structured in this country, everybody doesn't have a job, and the people that want work, can't work, most of them. But they (also) know often if they get a job, they got to hire a baby-sitter, they got to have carfare, they got to have clothes.[20]

The Bonanza in Beantown

Mothers on welfare in Massachusetts knew of these problems only too intimately. Their commitment to changing the system provided one of the more successful examples of organizing in the movement. By 1970, local NWRO affiliates (massed together in the Massachusetts Welfare Rights Organization—MWRO) had a combined recipient membership base of 4,000 women, and many more if their children were counted. Like the larger movement, MWRO built its base around the promise of immediate benefit rewards, rather than a vague justice in an indefinite future.

Originally organized in Boston's predominately African American section of Roxbury, Mothers for Adequate Welfare (MAW) began its work in the summer of 1965. In June 1967, several dozen members staged a sit-in at the local welfare office. When Boston Police intervened and violently removed the women from the building, three straight days of "disturbances" shook the city—a message to government bureaucrats about treating poor people with disdain.

Boston MAW was soon helped by traditional organizing techniques, led in part by Bill Pastreich, a white professional organizer. Soon, there were organized chapters of MAW in virtually every public housing project in the city. Many were involved in coordinated actions at welfare department offices in August 1968, where they demanded expanded benefits, and supplementary welfare checks for furniture and household appliances.

Fearing more "disturbances," nervous department officials

immediately released grants to almost every recipient taking part in the protests. What the state legislature called "Black Tuesday" (MWRO referred to it as "the bonanza") helped MAW recruit many more members in cities throughout the state.

New groups were organized "on almost an assembly line basis," Bill Pastreich noted later, as the "Boston model" of organizing was put into effect. It showed, as Lawrence Ballis wrote in *Bread or Justice,* that the "typical welfare recipient will make the sacrifices of time, energy and resources to join a self-help or lobbying organization if, and only if, she is convinced that doing so will bring her tangible benefits that are quickly realizable."[21]

Organizers going door to door to recruit new members would encounter negative attitudes about "militant" welfare recipients like "those crazy ladies from Roxbury" who had become so prominent in the local media. As Ballis points out, organizers were ready for these criticisms and would typically respond by saying something like this:

> Those ladies are a lot like you. They didn't want to get involved but their children need beds and clothing and they vowed not to leave the welfare office until they got it. It's only because of the actions of people like those ladies in Roxbury that furniture and clothing are available to you today.[22]

While most of the organizers related the personal benefits the campaign could bring to the recipient or tried to counter the inferiority many women felt about being on welfare, they also used conversations with recipients to communicate social change ideology and the need for power. As Ballis describes it, such an appeal sounded like the following:

> The reason welfare is so bad is because welfare recipients are not organized. One by one they can't get what they need because they have no power—and that's what this country responds to, power. The first kind of power is money power...The Welfare Department doesn't give us enough to live on. If we had money power, we wouldn't need the group so badly. The second kind of power is in the power of numbers. If we organize and get our people together, we can have that power to get what we need...and have the numbers to back us up in the Massachusetts Welfare Rights Organization and the National Welfare Rights Organization.[23]

Organizers in Springfield (Mass.) developed another pitch. They would go into recipients' homes and ask, "Where is your second chair? Do you have a chair for everyone in your family? Where is your couch? Do you have beds, sheets, pillows, pillowcases? These things are your rights," they'd say and leave a flyer announcing an upcoming meeting. Organizer Wade Rathke recounted the success of a protest at the welfare department:

> The ladies did the talking [to the welfare workers] and told them they would be back in exactly two weeks to pick up their checks. [Two weeks later] we appeared there and we must have had at least four hundred people. And by God, if we didn't get the checks for the children's special clothing allowance! It was like a hell of a great day for those recipients who were walking out of there with checks for a hundred, two hundred, or three hundred dollars. People could see that they had won, through organizing and being with NWRO and Springfield Welfare Rights. We were already talking about the next campaign to get furniture.[24]

Some of the demonstrations and actions were bold, even for the times. After more than 7,000 welfare mothers and their allies in Wisconsin marched to the capital, police geared up to protect the state assembly building. "Completing the final leg of the march," according to NWRO's newsletter *The Welfare Fighter,* "about 2,000 people stormed through the front door and forcibly entered the empty chambers of the state assembly, packing it to the walls."[25]

The last campaign in the welfare rights movement also was one its boldest. And it is the one that most resembles what today's community organizations are doing—fighting to keep things from getting worse. In 1971, the state of Nevada decided that the best way to reduce the surging welfare rolls was to purge recipients by making eligibility requirements more strict. Despite the glitter and abundance represented by Las Vegas and Reno, there was poverty in Nevada. As one of the most conservative states, it had ridiculously low welfare grants.

NWRO organized "Operation Nevada." More than five thousand protesters, recipients and other volunteers served notice that the state could not just cut more than half of its welfare roll without a response. At Caesar's Palace, demonstrators chanting "Welfare

Rights Now!" pushed their way into the lobby and took control of the ornate building. It was a media event like no other. The protests completely disrupted the Las Vegas Strip, scaring tourists and seriously damaging business income. Two days later, the state reversed itself and threw out the new policy. It was to be the welfare rights movement's last major victory.

Mounting Obstacles and Challenges

There were conflicts within NWRO about how best to organize and build a poor people's movement. The "Boston model" relied heavily on outside organizers, while what became known as the "Johnnie Tillmon model" emphasized reliance on the recipients themselves as both organizers and leaders; in that model, decision-making and authority rested with the women. Though both models could claim victories, the different ideologies caused tensions inside the movement that never went away.

The movement faced challenges as well. New York City established the flat grant system in August of 1968—which countered the demand for special grants with a simplified (but cost-cutting) one-time payment. Large protests ensued, with police taking a cue from Chicago's Finest during the Democratic Convention the same month, as mounted cops used nightsticks on many of the mostly Black and female demonstrators. "Screaming women charged that the police wouldn't do this to white people," the *New York Times* reported. Some commentators noted the similarity of these events to the history of the Bonus Marchers in Washington three decades earlier.[26]

Probably the biggest reason that welfare rights activity died was that local governments learned to respond by cutting off grants or instituting the "flat grant" system, which eliminated the potential to organize around "special need payment" grievances. Some organizers felt that recipients lost interest once they were able to get furniture and basic services. The solid base of support organizers had hoped to create that would work for an ideal of "economic justice" never materialized.

NWRO redirected its efforts to lobby against Nixon's 1970 Family Assistance Program (FAP), which proposed to provide all Americans with the hoped-for guaranteed income—but at a measly $1600 a year, far short of NWRO's proposed $6500. Depleted of members and resources, worn out strategically and reeling from the tragic death of Wiley (who drowned in a boating accident), NWRO closed its doors in 1975, about a decade after it had started.

Clearly, the political climate was changing too. At the national level, government dropped its rhetoric about fighting poverty. With Richard Nixon's ascension to the presidency, welfare became more unpopular than ever. His "Southern Strategy" of appealing to working class whites tapped into hostility over not only welfare, but most anything that was perceived as helping Blacks and other people of color. By 1972, Nixon could score huge political points by warning that if presidential challenger George McGovern were elected he would "put half the population on welfare." The slogan of his "anti-poverty" policy was "Workfare not Welfare."

Unafraid and Dignified — A Legacy

Still, the movement had done the extraordinary. For the first time, it forced the welfare system to make grants available to many more families that were eligible. In 1960, only about 750,000 families received AFDC. By 1972, that number was more than 3 million, an increase in benefits in excess of $5 billion.

Recipients were no longer subjected to demeaning and unannounced caseworker visits to their homes, fair hearings were conducted in matters of eligibility questions, and local welfare centers provided written and accessible guidelines about what folks were entitled to.

NWRO and the movement in general were highly instrumental in reshaping the food stamp program, initiating the school lunch program and spurring the creation of other nutritional and health programs for low-income people.

Most important to many was that the organizing recipients had done gave them courage, made them feel they had a stake in their own lives and that they could take control over their fates by working together. It also helped to foster the notion, at least temporarily, that those receiving public aid are human beings like everyone else and have the same aspirations for a dignified and productive life as nonrecipients. "For the first time in my life," said one recipient, "someone was telling me I'm a worthy human being. Welfare rights organizing made me feel like I could do almost anything I wanted to."[27]

"We were used to begging," said Ms. Halstrum, a recipient in New York City in the 1960s. "We never demanded anything—welfare rights enabled us to walk in a welfare center unafraid, dignified and secure in the knowledge that our needs would be met."[28]

"It was a revolutionary idea at the time," Tim Sampson recalls, "that the lowest rung of society's ladder could struggle for their rights. This struggle really opened people's eyes and made them realize like never before that they were entitled to their rights."[29]

As NWRO and the local organizations matured out of direct action welfare rights activity, many remained active in the fight for control of their lives, joining school and local hospital boards, political or neighborhood associations and parent-teacher organizations.

Today, in the absence of movement organizing, the welfare reform debate has been largely relegated to political posturing and legal maneuvering. While conservatives have argued that welfare should be abolished entirely, progressives have been painted into a political corner, stuck resisting further budget cuts instead of fighting for economic justice. The notion of "welfare rights" seems almost absurd to most in today's climate of open hostility toward those thought to be "getting a free ride."

Many years after the welfare rights movement, Johnnie Tillmon remarked that "in order to keep going and learning, it is always important to look back and remember."[30] Today the welfare struggle continues only on the local level across the country, but with the benefit of a rich legacy.

NOTES

1. Piven and Cloward, *Poor People's Movements,* p. 266–68.
2. Fisher, *Let the People Decide,* p. 35.
3. Kotz and Kotz, *A Passion for Equality,* p. 199, 235;
4. Tim Sampson, interview with author, San Francisco State University, March 1994.
5. Kotz and Kotz, p. 199.
6. Ballis, *Bread or Justice,* p. 8.
7. For a full explanation of the theory, see Piven and Cloward.
8. Kotz and Kotz, p. 185
9. Ibid, p. 190.
10. Ballis, p. 17.
11. Kotz and Kotz, p. 222.
12. Deborah Amos, interview with author, January 1994.
13. Pope, *Biting the Hand,* p. 14.
14. Ibid, p. 21.
15. Jackson and Johnson, *Protest by the Poor,* p. 13
16. Ibid, p. 55.
17. West, *The National Welfare Rights Movement,* p. 41.
18. Jackson and Johnson, p. 123.
19. West, p. 219.
20. Lipsitz, *A Life in the Struggle,* p. 166.
21. Ibid, p. 19.
22. Ibid, p. 38.
23. Ibid, p. 40–41.
24. Kotz and Kotz, p.228–29.
25. Jackson and Johnson, p. 40.
26. Pope, p. 96.
27. Ibid, p. 135.
28. Ibid, p. 99.
29. See note 4.
30. West, p. xi.

CHAPTER EIGHT

"No Evictions.
We Won't Move!"

The Struggle to Save the I-Hotel

"This land is too valuable to permit poor people to park on it."
—Justin Herman, former executive director of the
San Francisco Redevelopment Agency, 1970[1]

Some of the manong tenants of the International Hotel.   Photo by Chris Huie

The land Herman was referring to in the quote above was a city block in the heart of downtown San Francisco's growing Financial District. One of the most famous skylines in the world was being reshaped. The "Wall Street of the West" had been expanding for years and the 800 block of Kearny Street was prime real estate. It was also the block where the International Hotel stood.

And it became the block where the rights of people of color who were low-income and elderly tenants were fought over for nearly a decade. The movement to save the "I-Hotel," as it was called, is one of the most important chapters in the history of Asian American struggle and of housing conflicts. It was a protracted campaign that eventually drew hundreds of people into the ranks of activism. It was, as the *San Francisco Chronicle* put it, "a cause celebre for the politically engaged."[2]

In the late 1970s, the I-Hotel was just about all that was left of Manilatown, once a thriving community of mostly male Filipino immigrants that covered 10 blocks between San Francisco's Chinatown and Financial districts. During the 1920s and 1930s, the I-Hotel (built the year after the devastating 1906 earthquake) became home to thousands of seasonal Asian laborers. Many young Filipino and Chinese men who worked as day laborers, dishwashers, messengers and at any other profession that was deemed "appropriate for Orientals" lived there. So did old-timers, who settled in San Francisco following years of working in seasonal harvests, on merchant ships, in canneries in Alaska and Washington, and so on, up and down the Pacific Coast. Many of the old-timers, though not citizens, had served in both World Wars, but the U.S. government denied some of them promised benefits after the fighting stopped.

Asian women were, for the most part, excluded from entering the U.S. until 1965, thereby preventing most of the men who lived in Chinatown and Manilatown from establishing families. Further, California's antimiscegenation laws prevented Filipinos and other Asians from marrying outside the race. Nevertheless, "race preservation" was the concern of white elite California in the 1930s; testimony before the House Committee on Immigration and Naturalization warned that "the Filipinos are...a social menace as they will not leave our white girls alone and frequently intermarry."[3]

Yet a different kind of family life persisted, as the bachelor society of Filipino men preserved their culture in the pool halls, barber shops and other Manilatown meeting places. As one of the Filipino elders who lived in the I-Hotel remarked in 1987, "Have here a good neighborhood, and good and very kind country men, old and new friends.... I have stayed here so long that I call this hotel my home."[4]

"It was a good place for brown people—Filipinos—specifically coming for jobs in Alaska or on the farms—a unique place where you met friends to guide you and maybe recommend you for jobs," said longtime resident Nick Napeek.[5]

Fellow resident Peter Yamamoto echoed the sentiment:

> Living in the I-Hotel and Manilatown-Chinatown, you realize the need of Filipinos and Chinese to live within their community, where they could find the day-to-day things that they could not find living in, say, the Tenderloin—a cheap hotel, their food, their friends. [It] was a beautiful place, with camaraderie.[6]

Urban Renewal = Filipino Removal

After World War II, San Francisco made plans to expand its downtown business sector, particularly the area around the Financial District. Redevelopment was the buzzword of the time and more and more corporate headquarters moved into the area. As the high-rises went up during the building boom of the late 1950s and 1960s, many small businesses and residential hotels were torn down.

The city's spreading "urban renewal" project had already torn through the heart of the Fillmore District, west of downtown, decimating hundreds of homes and displacing thousands of residents in the city's largest Black community. But it was the Financial District redevelopment that became top priority for the city's expansion, as the opening of the Bay Area Rapid Transit system in the mid-1970s made it easier for white-collar workers to commute from the outlying areas into downtown to work in the major banks, trading companies and other corporate entities moving into the area.

The effect, of course, was to change the landscape of the community. Manilatown was devastated. Ten full blocks of low-cost housing, restaurants, barber shops, markets, clubs and other businesses that benefited a Filipino community that numbered around

10,000 people were destroyed.

By the end of the expansion, thousands of people had been displaced. More than 4,000 low-income units were torn down in favor of high-rise buildings (including the famous Transamerica Pyramid and the Bank of America's world headquarters) and parking lots. Four out of every five low-cost residential hotels in the area were gone by the end of the 1970s.

One of the hotels slated for demolition was the International Hotel, where tenants could rent rooms for only 50 dollars a month. In the late 1960s, most of the hotel's tenants were poor, and almost all were elderly—in the community they were referred to as manongs, an Ilocano term of respect for the "old-timers." One of the manongs, Felix Ayson, remarked in 1986, "Most of my time and my years in America I spend in this hotel, so it is my home. Whenever no work in the country, I come here and find a job in the city, and I live here." Ayson had lived in the I-Hotel since 1928.[7]

More than three million elderly people in America's cities depended on low-cost residential hotels in the 1950s and 1960s, but by the close of the 1960s, the hotels had become synonymous with urban decay and blight as politicians and investors sought to justify redevelopment.

In March 1968, Milton Meyer and Company, headed by San Francisco business magnate Walter Shorenstein, bought the I-Hotel and made plans to construct a multilevel parking lot on the site. Shorenstein secured a demolition permit in September, and in October he ordered the evictions of the 196 tenants, giving them until the first of the year to be out. "We deeply regret having to disrupt the lives of these good people," Shorenstein said as the eviction notices went out.[8]

In the dizzying pace of downtown redevelopment, the sale of the I-Hotel and the eviction notices to its tenants were barely noticed, except by a few, including Joaquin Legaspi, director of the Manilatown Information Center, a multiservice provider for the community. San Francisco State College professor Jovina Navarro, who had been active in the Filipino community, also learned of the evictions and put out the first word on the college campus, leading to a series of highly publicized protests, led by newly politicized

Asian American students at San Francisco State and UC Berkeley. At the time, students at both campuses were beginning to press for ethnic studies programs and were also in the midst of protests over the war in Vietnam.

Many students involved in the campus-based Third World Liberation Front sought to practice the principles espoused in their new ethnic studies and consciousness movements; the idea, a novel one on college campuses, was to go back into the community and work for justice. The early I-Hotel demonstrations became a political introduction for large numbers of Asian American students in search of their cultural roots.

"It was a generation of a lot of activism," recalled Terry Bautista, who was active in the defense of the manongs. "We were looking for our own voice. The I-Hotel struggle was a good application of what ethnic studies was all about—go study your community and look for justice where there isn't any. There was just so much going on at the time. You couldn't help but be political."[9]

"Fight to Save the I-Hotel" became a battle cry among young activists and organizers.

The sudden interest in the hotel and publicity from the community soon led to a change in direction; a lease agreement between Milton Meyer and Company and the United Filipino Association (UFA), led by Ness Aquino, was drawn up and plans to make the land into a parking lot were shelved. But before the agreement could be signed, a fire broke out in the building, killing three tenants and giving Shorenstein justification to cancel the agreement and go ahead with demolition.

Returning Resources to the Community

The community continued to resist demolition by staging increasingly loud demonstrations, and most of the elderly tenants, including some who had been at the hotel for more than 20 years, refused to leave. Eventually, the UFA secured a three-year lease agreement, promising to bring the building up to housing code standards within a year. Volunteers, mostly from UC Berkeley's Asian American Studies program, worked to refurbish the hotel. Floyd Huen, who headed the UC program, later recalled using student fees in the project and justifying it as "returning resources to the community."[10]

Over the next several years, the fight over who controlled the hotel was tied up in the courts. The UFA dissolved and in its place the International Hotel Tenants Association (IHTA) was organized, led by Emil de Guzman.

Bill Sorro, in his 20s at the time of the demonstrations but not a student, was the only young person living in the I-Hotel at the time. Between 1970 and 1974, he called the three-story building his home:

> I was just another tenant, I paid my $45 a month in rent, I mean, I had responsibilities there — I painted, cleaned bathrooms, really whatever needed to be done. I wanted to get involved in the Filipino community, so I knew the issues, but I really saw myself as another tenant...I related to the old-timers. I was part of them. They were like the relatives in my family. They were like my uncles, you know.
>
> People just focus on the big events and the evictions, but you have to understand that there were nine years of hard work that we put into that hotel. It was day-to-day, outside of the media spotlight, by a whole spectrum of people, across race and class lines. We really made good connections with the old-timers and were there for more than just demonstrations. We did all the related work that isn't very glamorous. We helped them understand their rights to Social Security and Medicare. I mean, these were immigrants and many of them just didn't know.
>
> Also, as part of our work as budding revolutionaries, we tried to figure out how to change the environment of the community of people in the hotel to see themselves as being part of more than just their locked-in building. We provided social activities, we got a bus from UC Berkeley and took them out for day trips to the beach to have a barbecue and that kind of thing. I think we really succeeded in developing a trust between the young people and the tenants. Now they may not have agreed with all of our revolutionary rhetoric, but they were like your grandparents. They understood your heart and showed a lot of patience with you. It was a special thing.[11]

The International Hotel had become a symbol of more than just a housing struggle. For the many people who became intimately involved with the residents and their community, the hotel became a matter of the heart. The folks who worked to bring the hotel back from the brink of destruction were also able to use the media to communicate that, after all, these were elders who were being threatened. Hotel organizers were able to sway public opinion and, as a result, make the city's political leaders feel the heat. It appeared as though the hotel was going to survive its most direct challenge.

Tired of the bad press and the extensive community support of the hotel at any mention of demolition, Shorenstein secretly sold it in 1973 to a Thai businessman named Supasit Mahaguna and his Four Seas Investment Corporation for just over $850,000. Four Seas applied for a demolition permit but was immediately met with more protests and litigation. Finally, in 1976, Superior Court Judge Ira Brown, a former San Francisco landlord himself, ruled in favor of Four Seas and ordered the evictions. San Francisco Mayor George Moscone attempted to broker a deal that would have the city buy the hotel and sell it back to the tenants, but at $1.3 million, the price was impossible.

Eventually, the eviction order stuck and the San Francisco Sheriff's Office and Police Department were ordered to re-post eviction notices.

No Evictions! We Won't Move!

Word spread among people who had initially defended the hotel and who had promised support if another attempt was ever made to kick the tenants out. For Asian American activists and organizers, who had been politicized in the heat of the first battle and were presently working in the community, word that eviction notices were going up was a beacon call.

On January 7, 1977, more than 350 supporters from the IHTA, Asian Community Center, Kearny Street Workshop and other community groups and organizations in solidarity with the tenants formed a human barricade to prevent the police from posting the notices. Chanting "No eviction! We won't move!" the demonstrators forced the city and the police into retreat. The next week, after notices were finally posted, some 5,000 people linked arms around the entire block to prevent the forced eviction of tenants. The show of resistance and "threat of violence" forced Judge Brown to grant an immediate stay of eviction. Brown cited unconfirmed reports that tenant supporters had been stockpiling automatic weapons and gasoline.

In May, however, a court ruling strengthened Four Seas' claim of ownership and eviction notices again appeared. Again they were met by massive demonstrations, including a night when another human fence grew eight people deep in front of the hotel. "We have been terrorized by insecurity and fear," tenant Felix Ayson shouted to supporters during the eighth eviction attempt in the now nine-year-long struggle. "We are here to fight for our right to stay!" Again, the tenants won a stay of eviction.[12]

On August 2, I-Hotel tenants Wahat Tampao, Nita Radar, Benny Gallo, Ayson and others conducted a sit-in at City Hall to pressure the mayor and Board of Supervisors to support the struggle. The next day, however, the conservative California Supreme Court lifted the stay and reordered the evictions. This time sheriff's deputies and city police came with a show of force stronger than before. Again they were met with resistance.

Terry Bautista remembers the duties of the young organizers leading up to the evictions:

> We all took on any assignments that were needed. Some were needed to work the phones. Some were lookouts on the roof. I remember 20 or more people sleeping on a stage inside the building, while large numbers of other people were helping the tenants. Some would stay with them in their rooms to make sure that nothing happened to them. My job was to be a lookout [for police] at the front door. It was basically sentry duty. The cops could come at any time and we had to be ready. It was like we were getting ready for war.[13]

The plan of action for the inevitable day when the police would come with full force was to form the largest human barricade possible, seven to eight rows deep around the block with even more people layered inside the building, up every step, outside every room. Even the Reverend Jim Jones (yes, *that* Jim Jones) of the People's Temple had mobilized more than 300 of his followers and arrived on the scene in seven busloads. "Just imagine, it was wall-to-wall people around the whole block," Bautista says. "It was a constant mass of protest. It really was incredible."

The police had cordoned off a two-square-mile perimeter to stop what probably would have been thousands more who intended to come to the hotel in support of the tenants.

Tenant Nick Napeek remembers getting home around 4 p.m. on the night of August 3. He had heard that the police were coming that night. Around 10 pm, he started telling the other, older tenants on his side of the building to go inside their rooms and lock up.

The riot police could be seen blocks away practicing maneuvers in full riot gear; a battalion of mounted police had their horses ready for action. Finally at 3 a.m. on August 4, the cry from somewhere in the crowd came: "They're coming!" Some 400 police in full riot gear rushed the 3,000-person-strong barricade to evict the 50 or so tenants barricaded inside the hotel.

The resulting scene, captured on film in Curtis Choy's moving documentary *The Fall of the I-Hotel,* was of demonstrators, who had been linked arm-in-arm, being forcibly moved out of the way, of police moving in and breaking down doors and of their brutality to some tenants who didn't move quickly enough for them. Tenant Tony Goolsby told *East-West,* "They threw us up against a wall in the middle of the building.... One told me, 'If you don't move, I'll break your fucking neck!'"[14]

San Francisco Sheriff Richard Hongisto, who had earlier spent five days in jail for contempt of court when he refused to carry out an eviction order, apparently had a change of heart by the time he was leading the line of cops into the hotel. In a dramatic moment, with cameras flashing all around him, Hongisto used a sledge hammer to break down doors to tenants' rooms.

The pictures of old immigrant tenants being forced out into the street were shown on newscasts across the country and in many places outside of the U.S. The entire spectacle, according to most observers, including those who had never supported the tenants' stand, was disgraceful.

Tenant Florentino Ragadeo, who had lived in the same room for more than 20 years after serving in the U.S. Army and surviving the Bataan Death March in World War II, reserved blame for the real culprits. "I do not blame policeman, not blame sheriff," he told *East-West* days after the evictions. "The judge! The mayor! I know that they are the ones who have the right to stop the eviction. Especially the owner of the hotel. Before you evict, you should find a place for the tenants...I'm crying all the time...It's not right."[15]

"It was like the Roman Legions coming after the Christians," recalled de Guzman. "It was incredible humiliation. We had these elderly men who had to drag themselves to the street, and they were suddenly homeless. A lot of the manongs didn't really live much longer. It's like their hearts were broken."[16]

Preserving Heritage and History

On the 10th anniversary of the eviction, de Guzman explained the importance of fighting back against the powerful interests who wanted the hotel gone from sight. "For me and many of us who were born and raised in San Francisco, who have a lot of memories of what Manilatown was like as a community where our own fathers, relatives and friends hung out, the real issue was not the eviction but the attempt to destroy our heritage. The hotel was part of that historical foundation which we wanted to preserve."[17]

For more than a decade, the struggle to preserve the I-Hotel and all that it represented often occupied center stage in San Francisco politics. The issues of low-income housing, the rights of the elderly and people of color and the fight against "urban renewal" ("people rights over property rights," was a slogan from the demonstrations) were all ingredients in a struggle that eventually captured international attention.

Though the battle against eviction was lost and the hotel destroyed two years later—its fine bricks, ironically, used in the construction of million-dollar homes in other parts of the Bay Area—the struggle lives on in spirit. Many of the young Asian Americans, who became activists during that effort, found an important issue they could truly identify with. Politicized by the movement, many have stayed to work in the communities they rediscovered in 1968. A real pan-Asian American political identity was formed and from the subsequent work of these and other activists came a plethora of community services designed to meet the needs of Chinese, Japanese, Filipino, Korean, Cambodian, Vietnamese and other Asian immigrant populations.

"These were old people," said Bautista who, twenty years later, is still active, serving on the national council of Filipino Civil Rights Advocates. "You had to have a certain level of sympathy for them. We knew that we had to be accountable to our community. The system wanted control and wasn't willing to just give it up. Even though the manongs were evicted, the system really didn't win. We weren't defeated in one important sense: We learned the lesson of fighting back."[18]

Bill Sorro continues to work as a committed organizer, these days for low-income tenants in San Francisco's Mission District. "We can look back at the I-Hotel," he said, "and say that 20 years later, the same principles apply. Back then we called it self-determination. Today it's community empowerment. Whatever you want to call it, it's the same idea. People have rights, tenants have rights. We have to recognize those rights and fight back when we get pushed around. For the tenants in Manilatown we said, we're going to organize, fight back. That we should never let go of. If we ever stop fighting, then we've really lost."[19]

Today, 20 years since the 50 elderly tenants were forced out of their homes to make room for a parking garage, the lot at Kearny and Jackson streets remains empty. Ironically enough, it was never made into a parking structure, as developers and the city could never decide on a suitable project. Called "the Hole" now by locals, it is a strange sight in an area where giant skyscrapers dominate the terrain. To many, though, the lot is not just wasted land, but a monument to protest and to organized community struggle.

Postscript: After years of negotiation and community support, plans have been formalized to design and build a new International Hotel, with construction scheduled to be completed by the end of 1999. Low-income elders are to move into the new 14-story structure, which will include space for a performing arts center and a school of the arts for young people in the community. The new hotel will also house the Manilatown Cultural Center and Museum, where community artifacts and history—including some from the old I-Hotel—will be on display. Each floor is to be named after a prominent former tenant and an interior wall will list the names of all those who were evicted.

International Hotel poster. Produced by the San Francisco Poster Brigade, circa 1977. Courtesy of the Asian Community Center Archive and Harvey Dong.

NOTES

1. Choy, *The Fall of the I-Hotel*, film.

2. *San Francisco Chronicle,* May 25, 1986.

3. Takaki, *Strangers from a Different Shore,* pp. 328-330.

4. *Asian Week,* August 7, 1987.

5. Ibid.

6. *San Francisco Chronicle,* May 25, 1986.

7. Ibid.

8. *San Francisco Chronicle,* March 17, 1968.

9. Terry Bautista, interview with author, August 3, 1997.

10. Wei, *Asian American Movement,* p. 106.

11. Bill Sorro, interview with author, August 4, 1997.

11. *Asian Week,* August 7, 1987.

12. *East-West,* August 6, 1977.

13. See note 9.

14. *East West,* August 6, 1977.

15. Ibid.

16. *San Francisco Chronicle,* August 1, 1997.

17. Ibid.

18. See note 9.

19. See note 11.

CHAPTER NINE

"You Are Now on Indian Land"

Native Americans Occupy Alcatraz

Indians proclaim Alcatraz Island Indian land.   Photo by Harlan Stelmach

Until 1969 most people thought of Native Americans—if they thought of them at all—only as the perpetual losers to the cowboys in Hollywood Westerns. Unless you lived near a reservation, real live Indians were a historical figment, vestiges of a past long dead.

That past suddenly came back to life on the island of Alcatraz, a tiny rock in the middle of San Francisco Bay.

In November 1969, more than 300 Native Americans from more than 50 tribes took boats to Alcatraz Island, home of the infamous but by then abandoned federal penitentiary. The landing was a highly visible symbolic protest intended to dramatize a history of injustice and to demand redress for stolen lands and broken treaties.

For more than a year and a half, the Indian occupation of Alcatraz captured headlines worldwide. Alcatraz became a rallying cry, inspiring new struggles from California to New York. Indeed, the modern Native American movement was born there.

According to historian Troy R. Johnson in *The Occupation of Alcatraz Island,* Indian people (Muwekma, Hukueko, Coast Miwok, Pomo, Wintun, Wappo, Maidu and Northern Yokut) had been going to Alcatraz for 10,000 to 20,000 years before Europeans ever caught a glimpse of the Golden Gate. The Ohlone looked upon Alcatraz as "a place of isolation or ostracism for those who had violated laws or taboos." Even after European settlement it remained generally untouched until President Millard Fillmore in 1850 ordered the island reserved for federal use, mainly as a defense installation.[1]

After that, many Indians were held as military prisoners on the island, the largest group being the Moqui Hopi in 1895. Their offense? The Hopi had rejected a U.S. government policy that stripped them of traditional religious and cultural practices; they also refused to send their children into the U.S. government schools designed to destroy their culture and force assimilation. In 1907, the island was officially transformed into a federal prison and it remained so until 1963. During that time it established a reputation as the most impenetrable, escape-proof prison ever built and was a one-time home to such notorious criminals as Al Capone, the Bird Man and Machine Gun Kelly.

Termination and Relocation

Ironically, it was the federal government's attempt to kick Native Americans off their reservations that planted the seeds of the Alcatraz occupation. In the 1950s the U.S. government instituted a policy known as "termination." Its purpose was to end the government's relationship with more than 100 tribes and bands, effectively nullifying historic treaty obligations that had established Indian reservations on almost 1.5 million acres. There were strong economic motives behind the new policy. It was estimated at the time that 23 Western tribes slated to be terminated were on lands that harbored a third of the nation's low-sulfur coal, more than 80 percent of U.S. uranium reserves and 10 percent of U.S. gas and petroleum reserves.

The people were encouraged to relocate to cities and assimilate into mainstream American culture. Indian people who chose to relocate under the program were given bus transportation to one of eight urban areas and promised job training, help in finding a job and other services in order to adjust to city life. Nearly 11,000 decided to take their chances on finding a decent job, leaving behind unemployment rates of up to 80 percent on the reservations. Most went to Los Angeles, Phoenix, Denver, Dallas, Cleveland and San Francisco.

Those who were moved to the San Francisco Bay Area joined those Indian World War II veterans who had also come to take advantage of the region's tremendous resources. But the thousands of Indians who moved into the Bay Area soon found the promises of milk and honey to be as fulfilling as the broken treaties that had steadily decreased the size of the land from which they had escaped. Many found themselves torn between two worlds: the urban scene with its promises of economic improvement and the memory of the reservation with its familiar cultural and family ties.

If relocation was also meant to dilute Native American political power, it had the opposite effect. As individuals from various tribes congregated in cities, they created Indian support services, organizations and gathering places. Indians from disparate tribes realized that their political problems were essentially the same. A pan-Indian identity began to emerge.

New political groups gradually formed. In the Bay Area alone, an array of about forty different social, religious and political organizations helped ease the transition to city life. Groups like United Native Americans and the National Congress of American Indians in the San Francisco Bay Area started calling for an end to the termination policy and for a new era of self-determination. Organizations like the Intertribal Friendship House in Oakland, the Four Winds Club, the San Jose Dance Club and the Tlingit-Haida Club offered services in an environment that reinforced cultural value systems. At places like San Francisco State College and UC Berkeley, new attention to ethnic studies encouraged the growing number of Native Americans in school under the G.I. Bill to take on nationalist identities.

These pan-Indian cultural movements coincided with a new spirit of political resistance. Occasional rumblings of protest could be heard across Indian country during this time. In upstate New York, Tuscaroras and Mohawks, led by Mad Bear Anderson, demonstrated in the 1950s and early 1960s in opposition to the construction of power plants near their land. In 1958, Anderson helped organize protests against land seizures on Mohawk land. More than 100 state troopers sent in to remove the protesters were met by nearly 200 men, women and children who blocked access to the land. After many arrests and tremendous publicity, the state and the power companies backed down.

Elsewhere that same year, several hundred Indians marched on the Bureau of Indian Affairs in Washington D.C. to protest the termination policy. Out West, the Pit River Indians in California, Nevada and Utah refused to give up their traditional lands in return for government money, and the National Indian Youth Council sponsored "fish-ins" in the Pacific Northwest to protest discriminatory treatment of Indian fishermen by the state of Washington's Department of Fish and Game.

Claiming Surplus Land

There was much bitterness in the Bay Area about the effects of the relocation program. Though they had been promised jobs, housing, medical care and vocational training, Indians of all backgrounds found themselves dumped in poor neighborhoods with nothing more than a little cash. Anger was mounting and people began to talk about doing something.

In San Francisco, a Sioux (Lakota) woman named Belva Cottier recalled how the idea of staging a demonstration at Alcatraz came to her:

> One morning I was reading the newspaper and there was this
> story that the government didn't know what to do with Alcatraz,
> which was [to be declared] surplus land after the federal prison

was discontinued. So I thought about the old Sioux Treaty of 1868, which entitled us to claim surplus land.[2]

On March 8, 1964, five Bay Area Sioux men, including Cottier's husband, Allen, landed on the rocky soil of the former penitentiary. Belva Cottier recalled that panic-stricken officials on the island telephoned the federal marshals: "There are Indians on the island, feathers, bells and all!" The next day's newspaper headlines announced the "Wacky Indian Raid."[3] The occupiers offered to buy the land for 47 cents per acre, the same amount the U.S. government had offered under the 1946 Indians Claims Commission for more than 65 million net acres taken from California Indians. Although the Indians were quickly sent back from Alcatraz, local Indian activists did not forget the 1964 "invasion." As the community matured politically, many began to see bigger possibilities in an Alcatraz takeover. Richard McKenzie, one of the 1964 Alcatraz invaders, said in a 1969 meeting at the San Francisco American Indian Center: "Kneel-ins, sit-ins, sleep-ins [won't] help us. We might have to occupy government buildings before things [will] change."[4]

Said one activist many years later, "Every time you crossed the Golden Gate Bridge or the Bay Bridge, you saw that little spot in the water and remembered. You thought: 'Those 20 acres and all those buildings, all empty, falling apart from neglect—and we have nothing."[5] In 1968 Alcatraz was officially declared surplus property. In October 1969 a fire destroyed the important San Francisco American Indian Center, a gathering place for many Indian organizations and a service center that met the needs of more than 30,000 Bay Area Indians. At the same time, the San Francisco Board of Supervisors endorsed billionaire Lamar Hunt's plan to redevelop Alcatraz Island for commercial purposes. But Indian activists like Adam Nordwall and Richard Oakes recalled the 1964 landing. Alcatraz was only a mile and a quarter from Fisherman's Wharf. You could practically reach out and grab it. The time was ripe to make a move.

Oakes, who was to become an early spokesperson for the landing, and others visited college campuses throughout California to recruit Indian students to help occupy Alcatraz. The speakers spelled out the hazards and the dedication and commitment it would take to stay on the island. But they also talked about what a success the occupation could be and "how much it would mean to all Native Americans" if they could gather themselves in this symbolic demonstration. At UCLA, 80 Indian students decided to drop their books and travel to San Francisco to participate.

Organizers decided that the landing on Alcatraz would promote not any one individual or tribe, but rather all Native Americans. They named their group Indians of All Tribes (IAT). On November 9, 1969 and again the following week, large squadrons of Native Americans landed on the abandoned property, announcing to the world, "We hold the Rock!" At the same time, they set out their demands: that the federal government restore tribal land claims across the United States based on treaty obligations and that the government grant them title to Alcatraz under provision of an 1882 act that stated that abandoned federal facilities be utilized for Indian schools. In support of the demands, they relied on the infamously bitter language of Title 25, U.S. Code: "In all trials about the right of property in which an Indian may be party on one side, and a white person on the other, the burden of proof shall rest upon the white person."[6]

The IAT released the following statement upon landing:

> We, the Native Americans, reclaim the land known as Alcatraz Island in the name of all American Indians by right of discovery. We wish to be fair and honorable in our dealing with the Caucasian inhabitants of this land, and hereby offer the following treaty: We will purchase said Alcatraz for $24 in glass beads and red cloth, a precedent set by the white man's purchase of a similar island about 300 years ago. We know that $24 in trade goods for these 16 acres is more than was paid when Manhattan Island was sold, but we know that land values have risen over the years.[7]

Another section of the proclamation described why the taking of Alcatraz was an obvious choice:

> We feel that this so-called Alcatraz Island is more than suitable as an Indian reservation, as determined by the white man's own standards. By this we mean that this place resembles most Indian reservations in that:
> 1. It is isolated from modern facilities, and without adequate means of transportation.
> 2. It has no fresh running water.
> 3. The sanitation facilities are inadequate.

4. There are no oil or mineral rights.
5. There is no industry and so unemployment is very great.
6. There are no health care facilities.
7. The soil is rocky and non-productive and the land does not support game.
8. There are no educational facilities.
9. The population has always been held as prisoners and kept dependent on others.

Further, it would be fitting and symbolic that ships from all over the world, entering the Golden Gate, would first see Indian land, and thus be reminded of the true history of this nation. This tiny island would be a symbol of the great lands once ruled by free and noble Indians.[8]

Finally, the proclamation spelled out the IAT's intended uses of Alcatraz, which included:

1) An educational "Center for Native American Studies"; 2) a "Spiritual Center" to teach "ancient tribal religious ceremonies and medicine"; 3) an "Indian Center of Ecology" to train and support people engaged in scientific research for the purpose of restoring the environment to its more natural condition; 4) another Indian training school to "teach Indian people how to make a living in the world"; 5) the development of an American Indian museum. Part of the museum "will present some of the things the white man has given to the Indian in return for the land and life he took: disease, alcohol, poverty and cultural decimation... Part of the museum will remain a dungeon, to symbolize both those Indian captives who were incarcerated for challenging white authority, and those who were imprisoned on reservations."[9]

Both the seriousness of the statement and its sarcastic humor made for exciting media coverage. Though there were hostile reactions in the press (the *San Francisco Chronicle* editorialized that "no culture worthy of the name could be expected to spring from such litter [as these Indians]"),[10] most media outlets were at worst curious about the takeover and at best sympathetic.

Richard Oakes told the Alcatraz caretaker that if he cooperated, the Indians would make him head of a provisional Bureau of Caucasian Affairs. Oakes also announced to the press: "We came to Alcatraz because we were sick and tired of being pushed around, exploited and degraded everywhere we turned in our country. We selected Alcatraz because it is a place we can call our own."[11]

Others echoed this sentiment. Alcatraz occupier Peter Blue Cloud remarked on the welcome many following waves of Indians felt at first arriving on the island:

> A huge bonfire is burning and we can see many figures moving about. An amplified voice booms at us, 'Indians only. If you aren't Indians, please keep going and don't try to land. If you are Indian, welcome to Indian land! Come ashore and join your brothers and sisters.'[12]

As signs went up proclaiming YOU ARE NOW ON INDIAN LAND and WARNING: KEEP OFF INDIAN PROPERTY, headlines across the globe announced the bold move. Never before had Indian unity been asserted so clearly and defiantly. Occupiers realized that they were not going to be removed anytime soon. They knew the government, then under attack for its handling of the war in Vietnam and particularly for the massacre of rural Vietnamese villagers by American troops at My Lai, was going to take a kid-gloves approach. Those who thought that the military would come to remove them were philosophical. Dennis Turner, a 22-year-old Shoshone, said, "We won't resist, but how will they find us? It's why we are here in the first place—we are the invisible Americans."[13]

At Home on the Big Rock

The Indian occupiers recognized that they could only achieve their demands as long as they had a position of strength, and that meant maintaining the physical occupation for as long as possible. As the weeks stretched into months, Alcatraz became home to hundreds of Native Americans. Sleeping quarters were everywhere. Some stayed in the solitary-confinement cells, others in the chapel, the warden's house and the guards' quarters.

The group agreed that decisions would be made by an elected council of leaders from various tribes and nations. They included many who had planned the occupation: Oakes, Grace Thorpe, Al Miller, Ross Harden, Bob Nelford, Dennis Turner, Judy Scraper, LaNada Boyer and Charles Dana, to name a few. All represented themselves as IAT council members to the press.

In December the Big Rock School opened on the island for the children who were now living with family members. Continuing education for adults and many other services were also implemented in the early months of the occupation, and the island community functioned smoothly. Logistical problems abounded. There had been only three functioning toilets on the island, but an Indian plumber offered his services to the IAT and within a couple of weeks had 35 in working order.

One of biggest problems was getting supplies to feed and clothe the inhabitants and otherwise make life bearable on the rocky, freezing cold island. Adam Fortunate Eagle, then Adam Nordwall, writes about the support network in his book, *Alcatraz! Alcatraz!* Organizing "on the supply line" meant securing donations, equipment, boat transportation and health care. Hundreds in the Bay Area and beyond donated their time, energy and resources. Dr. Dorothy Lone Wolf Miller, a Blackfoot Indian, allowed her medical offices in San Francisco to be used as occupation headquarters and coordinated health and emergency services. When later federal research grants for her professional work were cut off as a result of her visible support she said, "What the hell! It was the price I had to pay for freedom."[14] Others like her formed what was without question the key role in making sure the occupation would work for more than a couple of weeks.

What began as a symbolic gesture to show Indian frustration with federal treatment of Indian people soon grew into a protracted battle of wills. In the summer of 1970, the government cut off phone, water and electrical service to the island, making life difficult for many of the families, especially those with young children and elders.

One of the occupiers, Shirley Keith, proclaimed the IAT's determination to stay: "We reject the fact that your government thinks it can legislate us out of existence, with complete disregard for the Indian people's treaty rights, tribal rights, human rights, civil rights and other rights—not privileges, rights—and that is why we are staying and we are not moving."[15]

The best offer the government would make (they called it their "maximum counter-proposal") involved turning Alcatraz into a national park with an "Indian quality" theme; Indians would be hired as park rangers and work under the supervision of the Department of the Interior. It didn't take long for the IAT to reject the insulting proposal.

Fear of repression by the police and U.S. officials could not deter the young activists, according to historian Troy Johnson, who wrote, "The federal government could not take anything away from them because they did not own anything."[16]

Alcatraz! Alcatraz!

The occupation of Alcatraz Island lasted 19 months and nine days. Its end came as the result of several factors, not least of which was internal dissension. Tragically, Richard Oakes' 13-year-old daughter Yvonne was killed when she fell down a stairwell in an empty building on the island. Activists in the mainland community who had known of dissension within the occupation believed Yvonne's death was not accidental and pointed fingers at a faction allied against Oakes. Several fires broke out on the island, destroying much property and causing further divisions among the remaining occupants. There was much blame to go around. Of course, the government's own "secret war" to infiltrate, discredit and "neutralize" militant movements also played a big role.

The end was unceremonious enough. Federal marshals, heavily armed, removed the last protesters from the island in June 1971 and put them on Coast Guard cutters back to San Francisco.

But Indian people could claim victory. They had managed to elevate the concerns of their communities as never before. Wilma Mankiller, who would later become the first woman chief of the Cherokee Nation, was a San Francisco State College undergraduate in 1969. In her autobiography, she describes the occupation of Alcatraz as an awakening that changed the course of her life:

> I'd never heard anyone actually tell the world that we needed somebody to pay attention to our treaty rights, that our people had given up an entire continent, and many lives, in return for basic services like health care and education, but nobody was honoring those agreements. For the first time, people were saying things that I felt but hadn't known how to articulate. It was very liberating...Alcatraz articulated my own feelings about being

an Indian. It was a benchmark. After that, I became involved.[17]

"Alcatraz! Alcatraz!" became a rallying cry for Indian protest and an inspiration for other campaigns. During the following five years there were more than 60 occupations of government land and buildings, including the Bureau of Indian Affairs headquarters in Washington. Alcatraz also gave birth to the Trail of Broken Treaties (see Chapter 11) and inspired the Longest Walk in 1985. In short, the occupation of Alcatraz was the catalyst for much of the Native American movement and cultural renewal that exploded in the 1970s and continues to this day.

While conservative sentiment—including some in Indian Country—looked upon the Alcatraz occupiers as spoiled college kids out to make a name for themselves and have a party at the same time, there is no denying what the drama on the island meant, both symbolically and in practical terms. Without the theater, it is doubtful anything could have commanded the instant attention the occupation brought to issues long ignored. The militancy of the campaign did more than all the conferences, meetings and political lobbying could ever have hoped to do.

Today, thousands gather for the annual "anti-Thanksgiving" protest on Alcatraz Island.
Photo by Harlan Stelmach

Although Washington will not admit it, the drama played out at Alcatraz and the movement it inspired helped to stop the hated termination and relocation programs and to start a new "self-determination" policy. The government returned Blue Lake and 48,000 acres to the Taos Indians in New Mexico, Mount Adams to the Yakima in Washington, 60,000 acres to the Warm Springs tribes, and more land to Navajo and Washoe tribes, among others, in the early 1970s.

In the end, the joke was on the government. Native Americans never really wanted to keep the island anyway. Alcatraz is now home only to its indigenous inhabitants—the birds.

NOTES

1. Johnson, *The Occupation of Alcatraz Island*, p. 2-4.
2. Ibid, pp. 17–18.
3. Ibid.
4. Ibid, pp. 19, 36–37.
5. Ibid, p. 50.
6. Churchill and Vanderwall, *Agents of Repression*, p. 119.
7. Eagle, *Alcatraz! Alcatraz!* pp. 44–45.
8. Ibid.
9. Ibid, pp. 46–47.
10. Quoted in Smith and Warrior, *Like a Hurricane*, p. 109.
11. Johnson, p. 65.
12. Ibid, p. 115.
13. Ibid, p. 69.
14. Eagle, p. 78.
15. Smith and Warrior, p. 27
16. Ibid, p.49.
17. Mankiller and Wallis, *Mankiller*, p. 191–193.

CHAPTER TEN

Participation with Power

Parents Fight for Community Control of New York City Schools

In any community, one of the things parents care about most is the quality of the education available to their children. In many cities and towns, however, making schools better is an uphill battle against lack of money, dilapidated buildings, and outdated curriculum materials. Even worse, the school system itself is sometimes part of the problem, particularly in communities of color, which have often received "separate and unequal" educational services.

When parents mobilize, however, they quickly realize that to succeed, they have to take some of the school district's power for themselves. One classic battle over school control occurred in a Black and Puerto Rican neighborhood of New York City's Brooklyn borough known as Ocean Hill-Brownsville. Between 1966 and 1968, parents and community organizers in Ocean Hill-Brownsville fought the school system and the teachers union to a standstill in their efforts to improve education for their children.

In New York City's public schools in the second half of the 1960s, a million kids were crammed into classrooms that were typically dirty and overcrowded. Of the large numbers of Black and Puerto Rican students, only about half finished high school. Reading levels were far below the national average. The main advice doled out to the young women and men about life after graduation was "Don't get pregnant" or "Join the military." College was out of the question. Expectations all around were extremely low.

More than a decade after the Supreme Court's landmark 1954 *Brown v. Board of Education* decision outlawing segregated public schools, the sad fact of "separate and unequal" education in cities around the country was beginning to receive some national attention. The problem could no longer be blamed on the backward South. "It was racism, northern-style, that we had to deal with," said the Reverend C. Herbert Oliver, whose kids were failing in the New York City schools after they had done well in the South. "Bureaucratic racism. It was institutionalized in the North, but more disguised."[1] Even James Allen, the New York State Commissioner of Education had concluded by 1964 that nothing was being done as a result of *Brown* to seriously alter the terrible conditions in the city's public schools.

Many Black and Latino families in New York, already all too familiar with the situation, were further agitated when plans to ease overcrowding at Intermediate School (IS) 201 in Harlem were shelved because of budget problems. In addition, no Puerto Ricans or Blacks were among those hired as new teachers or the new principal. One parent organizer, Helen Testamark, suggested that because the city was incapable of satisfying parent concerns, the community should be given the chance to run the school. "Let us pick the principal and the teachers," she said. "Let us set the educational standards and make sure they are met."[2]

By the late 1960s, parents were beginning to take charge in several communities. Mobilization for Youth, a community group based in the heavily Puerto Rican and Black Lower East Side, was organizing mothers to challenge their kids' suspensions from school. Things were stirring in Harlem, too, and throughout the city. Quality education was becoming a civil rights call.

In December 1966, a group of parents and community organizers from around New York City conducted a sit-in at the Board of Education. They were fed up with how overcrowded the schools were, how little actual learning was taking place—"nobody ever got homework," they said—and the way teachers tended to either ignore the mostly Black and Latino students or discipline them inappropriately. Children who were considered to have "behavior problems" would be assigned to special education classes, which removed them from academic classrooms to ones where they were simply baby-sat.

Dolores Torres, a Puerto Rican mother whose three children and one niece attended schools in the Ocean Hill-Brownsville section of Brooklyn, recalled:

> We would lodge complaints and nothing was done about it. One night, we went down there for a meeting, and they started turning off the mikes like they usually did, and we just took over. We took their seats....it was a dramatic thing, but it was something that had to be done. Because we had no voice power. If you have kids in the school system and they aren't being taught, then eventually you're just going to rebel. We just kept saying, "Well, they're not representing us. Maybe we should represent ourselves."[3]

During the fall of 1966, Harlem parents boycotted IS 201; similar boycotts spread throughout other poor Latino and African American neighborhoods in New-York. As in Ocean Hill-Brownsville, no one from these communities sat on the local district school boards. As the boycotts spread, so too did the idea of real community control over the schools.

Faced with continuous pressure on its board of education, the city decided to create three "demonstration districts" in which some of the decision-making and functions of the schools would be decentralized, putting them ostensibly in the hands of the community. Ford Foundation grants totaling more than $150,000 were earmarked for planning, hiring and other logistical matters related to this innovative program. There was also money earmarked for "community participation," which was translated into hiring ten people to canvass neighborhoods and organize parents.

The experimental districts were to be at IS 201 in Harlem, Two Bridges on the Lower East Side (a mainly Chinese and Puerto Rican neighborhood), and Ocean Hill-Brownsville, the neighborhood connecting Bedford-Stuyvesant and Brownsville in Brooklyn. The experiment of decentralization was a community-led, city-sponsored effort at redistributing power, mainly from the professional teachers and administrators to the parents and the community. Parent participation meant nothing, many said, unless parents had a say in any changes made. As the saying went, "Participation without power is a ritual."

At Ocean Hill-Brownsville, parents elected a governing board made up of parents, community activists, clergy and teachers. This board was to have final authority over the key areas of school policy, including budget matters, curriculum and personnel, at eight different sites. Hiring decisions no longer would come only through the civil service staffing agencies, and the board succeeded in hiring community folks determined to improve their kids' education.

The board also appointed an eighteen-year veteran of the New York school system, Rhody McCoy, as unit administrator. Prior to the appointment of McCoy, there had never been an African American superintendent of public schooling in America's largest city. McCoy made it clear early on that he was not there just for cosmetic purposes. He supported the parents in their struggle against the bureaucracy. McCoy criticized teachers for not responding to community members with respect, charging that, "when parents protest, you look down on them." He truly valued support from the community in making the schools better. Meetings between teachers, the governing board and the community were open and they were frequent.

"It was a joy to go to a board meeting," McCoy recalled in an interview for the television documentary *Eyes on the Prize* twenty years later. "Not only were the board members present, but the community folk were sitting around, and they had as much input as the board. And it was always on a positive note—'how do we help the youngsters?'"[4]

Ninety percent of the teachers in New York City schools were white, while 95 percent of the students in Ocean Hill-Brownsville were Black or Latino. Most teacher complaints were about the students lacking discipline and being disruptive, how difficult it was to control the students and how their jobs felt like "combat duty." Many in the community took those complaints to mean that most white teachers had no way of dealing with the students except as adversaries. The local board therefore made it a priority to recruit and hire more teachers who looked like the students they would be serving. By the 1967-68 school year, the board had assembled a much more diverse faculty and staff.

Benny Wilkinson, a Black high school student, talked about how students had seen school as demoralizing:

A lot of the teachers really didn't know what they were teaching. You could say they wasn't interested in their jobs enough to help out anybody. You know, like go to them and ask them a question about this and that and the other, and they would say, "Ah, well, right now I have to do this and I can't answer." But they didn't ever come around to answering it at all. The school itself has a real bad reputation. So that a lot of the teachers there, they just normally think, "Okay, these kids are not going to care anyway. So I don't have to do this." So after a while you just lose interest.[5]

Rev. Oliver, who was chair of the governing board, noted the importance of bringing in teachers who knew the community. "We found that most of the teachers in the district came into the district, taught, and then went out of the district to their homes. And, of course, this is altogether different from the southern situation, because in the South, the teachers lived among the people. And the principals—all Black—lived somewhere among the people, and you got to know them."[6]

Karriema Jordan, who was in the eighth grade at Junior High School (JHS) 271 in 1968 rembers:

[With so many new black teachers at JHS 271], you learned a lot more. You identified more. You learned that teachers were human beings, not some abstract something. They stayed after school. At three o' clock, they didn't run downstairs and punch out. You know, they gave you more time. I mean, you felt more accepted. You weren't an outsider in your own school. They were part of your environment. I mean, they were Black. You can identify with them and they can identify with you. It's as simple as that. There's no big mystery, you know.[7]

One veteran teacher in Ocean Hill-Brownsville was amazed at the change in teacher attitudes.

When these new teachers arrived you could feel the difference. There was much less tendency to prejudge the children. The new teachers looked upon them as a group of kids who had to be taught, not as ghetto children who probably couldn't learn much. When I taught in this school a few years ago, teachers in the lounge talked mostly about their husbands, furniture, house—that sort of thing. Now most of the talk here is about how to teach these kids.[8]

At first, the teachers' union, the United Federation of Teachers (UFT), backed the idea of demonstration districts. But when the Ocean Hill-Brownsville board began to assert some control over who was going to be teaching in the schools, the powerful union and much of its rank-and-file got nervous. Led by Albert Shanker, the UFT had emerged in the early 1960s as a force to be reckoned with, as it won improved pay and job security for teachers throughout New York and then in other states and cities. But the Shanker-led UFT also opposed much of what McCoy and the community had set in motion.

"To me," said Shanker, who died in 1997, "the Civil Rights Movement was a movement for integration and a movement to eliminate segregation. In a sense, this [community control experiment] represented a kind of backward step. It represented a step by people in the community saying, 'We've given up on integration, so we want to take hold of our own schools.'"[9]

Some of the tenured faculty who had never supported the decentralization plan were not too happy to be taking direction from Black administrators and parents, and resisted many of the board's plans, including curriculum changes.

Torres, who became one of the board members, recalls the difficulty in getting cooperation from some teachers. "We were asking teachers to make an extra effort to get along with our kids, to teach our kids. If there was any problem, to possibly visit in the homes. Well, this wasn't in their contract. They didn't have to do these things. We had bells ringing at three o' clock for dismissal and teachers were out of there before the kids were."[10]

In the five years before the community districts were set up, only 12 teachers from the more than 60,000 employed by the city had been fired. The teachers' union was strong, and the Board of Education placed little importance upon the complaints of parents and students.

Towards the end of the demonstration school year, in May 1968, the Ocean Hill-Brownsville board transferred 13 teachers and five assistant principals from the district, all of whom had shown hostility in one form or another to what the community was trying to accomplish. In most school bureaucracies, transfers are not uncommon; if a teacher is having problems in a school, or if there is friction among faculty and staff, the Board of Education has no problem in putting transfers together. But when these 18 were moved out, all hell broke loose.

The UFT immediately protested the transfers, which they called "firings," and tried to get some of the teachers from Junior High School 271 to return. Flanked by police, the teachers were met with a barricade of angry parents and other community people. "We, the teachers, have to take steps to keep these people from miseducating our kids," Torres said at the time.[11] Right before the school year ended, 350 UFT members walked out of their classrooms in Ocean Hill-Brownsville to support the dismissed teachers.

At the beginning of the next school year in September, the board still refused to accept the teachers back, prompting the UFT to call a citywide teachers' walkout. Between then and Thanksgiving, three separate strikes kept all 57,000 teachers and more than a million kids out of school for eight weeks. The UFT and Shanker wanted the city to abandon the decentralization program completely, claiming the need for "due process" for the dismissed teachers as the pretext to regain control.

Some teachers, however, refused to uphold the strike, declaring that they would rather cross the picket line and honor the community and schools than a UFT leadership they felt had no interest in seeing children of color excel. The UFT claimed that it had the support of its rank-and-file Black and Puerto Rican teachers, but were proven wrong when Black and Latino caucuses were set up within the union and many from them crossed picket lines. Longtime Black teachers like Al Vann, Les Campbell, and Edgar Morris, and Puerto Rican teachers and principals like Louis Fuentes made it clear that they were not supporting Shanker and the UFT.

"I came into the district because I wanted to be accountable to the community," said Morris. "If I'm not doing the job, then I want them to kick me out. See, this is the only way to bring about any change. We have to be accountable to someone. In the New York City school system, it's no problem. Nobody ever gets fired."[12]

The UFT strike succeeded in creating more solidarity among Blacks and Puerto Ricans. Where there had been rivalries, the two communities began to see their common situation vis à vis "the powers that be." In the Black community, "the strike was a unifying factor," said Jitu Weusi later, who was then known by the name Les Campbell, an "Afro-American history" teacher in the district who had been suspended in another district for taking students to a service to commemorate Malcolm X's assassination. "Whether you were CORE, the Urban League, the Black Panther Party, the NAACP, you could rally around the issue. Everybody understood the importance of Black children receiving a quality education."[13]

Some schools were kept open during the strike. In Harlem, IS 201 opened every day and attendance was always high. Sound trucks would regularly pass thorough the neighborhoods informing people that the school was remaining open. Though custodians stayed away and refused to give up their keys, the teachers and parents managed to pry open the doors and break the locks. Cooperation between the students and community volunteers kept the schools clean and in good order. "You had a change in the learning atmosphere," McCoy recalled. "No more hooky, no more truant playing. Everybody was coming to school."[14]

Daily scenes in front of several schools in the district resembled pictures from the South's violent desegregation years, when police and the National Guard were brought in to keep competing sides from killing each other. Teachers' picket signs reading "End Mob Rule in Our Schools" and "Stop Teaching Racism" infuriated Latino and Black parents. Scuffles broke out and, as television cameras rolled, it looked like Little Rock had come to Brooklyn.

Karriema Jordan recalled:

> We had to go through barricades to get to the school. We'd look out on the rooftops, across the street from the school; the cops were there with their riot helmets and their nightsticks and helicopters, and the playground was converted into a [police] precinct, and walking up to the school you have just mass confusion. You have the community people out there. You have the UFT. You have the Black teachers on the inside. You were just amazed. You couldn't believe this was happening, you know, and you just went to school.[15]

In school, there was a new emphasis on studying Black and Latino historical and cultural perspectives. Curriculum changes were many and varied. Social studies classes, for example, challenged students to think critically about race relations; history classes covered the achievements and contributions of Latinos and African Americans and questioned European-centered concepts;

music classes incorporated African rhythms and indigenous Native American and Caribbean sounds; literature courses focused on Langston Hughes instead of Shakespeare, and so on.

"They (teachers) broadened our perspective," Jordan said. "[We began reading] DuBois, Malcolm X, even Mao Tse-Tung. We became international, which was a good thing because we were the Third World and the Third World is much larger than European history."[16]

Weusi was inspired by his memories of community support.

> There was a feeling of jubilation, and the parents and the community were so much behind us and so supportive of us...I used to walk through the streets of Ocean Hill at that time, and it was so beautiful. Parents used to come up and tell me to come in the house and have some fish or have some chicken or a cold drink. These were parents who were pouring their hearts out to people who they felt were doing something to educate their children.[17]

But the UFT didn't see it that way. They placed large ads in the *New York Times* charging the schools with "Black and Spanish racism" and teaching of "hate Whitey." Shanker called African American community activists "Black gangsters." Not only were most New York City teachers white, many were Jewish, and charges of anti-Semitism were levied against the "militants of Ocean Hill-Brownsville."

Even some of the dismissed white teachers were uncomfortable with the racism directed at the Ocean Hill-Brownsville organizers. Fred Nauman, one of the Jewish teachers given his transfer assignment from Ocean Hill-Brownsville, reported that he was seen as a hero by some. "We got some very negative support from various racist groups," he said. "I spoke at a couple of schools out in Bay Ridge, where they wanted me to run for political office. The thing that you heard was, 'You got the guts. You put the Blacks in their place.' It was disturbing."[18]

Several Jewish teachers crossed the picket lines. Charles Isaacs, a Jewish teacher at JHS 271, never wavered in his support for the program. "A year ago, I never thought that I would be crossing picket lines today," he said in 1968. "I have always supported unions. I have been called everything from 'scab' to 'Commie bastard' to 'nigger-lover lout.' [One letter I received] placed the hopes of the Jewish people in not producing any more like myself."[19]

After the first few weeks of the strike, the Board of Education ordered the Ocean Hill-Brownsville board to reinstate the teachers. But the word from the Superintendent fell upon deaf ears and the community rallied around the schools again. In early October, the Superintendent suspended the Ocean Hill-Brownsville community board and fired McCoy. Huge demonstrations followed in each of the city's five boroughs. People of all ethnic backgrounds carried banners protesting the policies of the city and the union as "Educational Colonialism." The last of the strikes was finally settled in mid-November.

Though the demonstration-district experiments were abandoned, the heightened sense of awareness in their own capacity led many active in the community control struggle to keep up the fight for educational reform. Weusi, for one, founded the private Uhura Sasa School in Brooklyn, but a private school is difficult to maintain in cash-strapped communities. Many continue to look to the public school arena for meaningful change.

Thirty years after Ocean Hill-Brownsville, a "new" approach to public education has emerged in the form of "charter schools"—schools organized and controlled by the cooperative efforts of parents and teachers. In 1996, one of these so-called "New Vision Schools" was being set up in Brooklyn. Called the Chaney, Goodman and Schwerner Leadership Academy (after the civil rights workers murdered in Mississippi in 1964), it intended to offer much of the orientation to learning that the Ocean Hill-Brownsville folks set in motion. Community participation is its key ingredient. Perhaps it is an idea whose time has finally come.

The union response and the sell-out by the city underlined the difficulties of working within the structures of public education. Yet, the troubling fiscal realities of creating a network of independent schools make parents dependent on the public schools, and on the hope that reforms like desegregation and court-ordered busing will provide the remedy. Through the Ocean Hill-Brownsville experience and others, communities of color have shown that greater changes are needed to create effective, relevant and meaningful education for their children, an education that gives a measure of power and control to the people whose destiny is in its hands.

NOTES

1. Hampton and Fayer, *Voices of Freedom,* p. 489.
2. Berube and Gittell, *Confrontation,* p. 26.
3. Carson, Garrow, et al., *Eyes on the Prize Civil Rights Reader,* pp. 361-62.
4. *Eyes on the Prize,* television series.
5. Wasserman, *The School Fix,* p. 411.
6. Hampton and Fayer, p. 489.
7. Carson, Garrow, et al., p. 377.
8. Fantini, Gittell and Magat, *Community Control,* p. 246.
9. Hampton and Fayer, p. 489.
10. *Eyes on the Prize.*
11. Ibid.
12. Ibid.
13. Ibid.
14. Hampton and Fayer, p. 497.
15. Carson, Garrow, et al., p. 370.
16. *Eyes on the Prize.*
17. Carson, Garrow, et al., p. 374.
18. Hampton and Fayer, p. 501
19. Carson, Garrow, et al., p. 374

CHAPTER ELEVEN
Back to the Blanket

The Trail of Broken Treaties Marches on Washington

The United States signed nearly 400 treaties with Native American nations—and broke every one of them. Despite the sacred words of the U.S. Constitution, which honors the power of the treaty above all other laws, Indian people have been the victims of some of the worst violations imaginable—from massacres to stolen lands to forced removal. But Native Americans did not forget the broken treaties, and in the 1960s and 1970s a new generation of Indian fighters decided to make good on past wrongs and be victims no more.

At first, the "Red Power" voice of the era was mostly rhetorical and coming from frustrated urban-dwelling Indians. This began to change, however, with the 1969 Indian occupation of Alcatraz Island in San Francisco Bay (see Chapter 9). Led by Indians of All Tribes (IAT), Alcatraz moved Indian movement tactics in the direction of militant direct action. In addition, the Alcatraz occupation framed the demand for the restoration of tribal lands in the context of the treaty provisions that had guaranteed it.

Reconnecting to the Reservation

In the early 1970s, the American Indian Movement (AIM) and other rapidly growing urban-based Native American organizations began to make connections with people back on the reservations; political activity accelerated at a furious pace. AIM was founded in 1968 in St. Paul, Minnesota by urban-based Indians recently released from prison. Having been politicized behind bars and inspired by some of the self-determination work of groups like the Black Panther Party, folks like Dennis Banks, Clyde and Vernon

Bellecourt and others decided to fight back against police violence, which, if you were Indian, was an ever-present reality. Wearing red jackets and armed with police radios, tape recorders and cameras, AIM activists followed the police to crime scenes involving Native Americans to monitor the treatment of Native Americans. They soon incurred the wrath of police authorities and the affection of the community. AIM membership took off in the Twin Cities and AIM chapters sprouted up across Indian Country.

At the same time, many Native Americans were growing up in large cities around the nation. Their parents had been subjected to a federal relocation program that the government said would help them find gainful employment and opportunities. According to Indian activists, however, the main purpose of the relocation program was to strip reservation-based Indians of any remaining power to oppose mining on their land and resist the government that protected the mining companies' interests. Many of the young Indians were politicized on campuses and in community centers in the cities, however, and sought the reservation as a place "to go back to the blanket." As a result, the revitalization of Indian culture was flourishing on the reservation and, politically, young activists looked there for inspiration from their communities. They also looked for issues to organize around.

Early in 1972, several incidents added to the tension surrounding Indian organizing. To activists, the U.S. government's war on militant organizing was not a secret, but it was many years before the facts emerged concerning the FBI's Counter-Intelligence Program (COINTELPRO). Not unlike the infiltration and provocation with which it plagued the Black Panther Party and other radical community-based organizations, COINTELPRO went after AIM and the growing Indian movement in general. By the summer of 1972, violence—official and otherwise—against Indian activists had increased dramatically both in the cities and on the reservation. The racially motivated murders of Raymond Yellow Thunder and Phillip Celay at the hands of whites that summer seemed to add urgency to the call across Indian Country for action.

A number of Indian organizers met in 1972 at Leonard Crow Dog's home on the Rosebud Sioux reservation in South Dakota to discuss a plan to gather Indians from around the country for a march into Washington D.C. Robert Burnette, the former tribal chairman at Rosebud, wanted to use such a march to demand federal attention to the poor living conditions Indians faced, and to force changes in the system of corrupt local tribal councils accountable more to the government's Bureau of Indian Affairs (BIA) than to tribal members.

Late in the summer, another larger group of activists met in Denver. It became apparent that there was general agreement among Indians in every section of the country for a march. Organizers began to formulate ideas for a caravan to be called "The Trail of Broken Treaties." The idea was to build both excitement and publicity along the cross-country trek, timed to culminate with the presentation of a list of demands to both presidential candidates in the week before the 1972 election. "We want to focus on the issues, and not on teepees near the Capitol dome," said organizer Hank Adams. "We don't want anything to detract from our focus on human lives." The caravan's other goal was to expose the corruption inside the BIA. "[The government] is pawning Indian land, bouncing checks all over the country, while the BIA takes the three-monkey position—hear no evil, see no evil, speak no evil," said Burnette, now co-chair of the march.[1]

Just as the violence of the summer had motivated many to act, another tragedy gave the plans for the caravan even greater intensity. In September, movement organizers learned of the murder of Richard Oakes, the charismatic Mohawk who had been the spokesperson and one of the leaders of the Alcatraz occupation a few years earlier.

The Caravan Marches

With Oakes' memory in mind, the caravan took off in early October. Three different West Coast contingents left from Seattle, San Francisco and Los Angeles and took routes through most of the Indian communities west of the Mississippi. The different caravans stopped in places of historic importance, like the sites at the Sand Creek and Wounded Knee massacres, locations of famous resistance in the Southwest, and at Mankato, Minnesota, known for its mass execution of thirty-eight Sioux warriors in 1862, the largest execution in U.S. history. Another caravan took off from Oklahoma and retraced the route of the bitter forced march of the Cherokee from their homeland in 1838 that became known as the Trail of Tears. Paul Chaat Smith and Robert Allen Warrior quote the plan for the caravan:

> [It will] be led by spiritual leaders who will carry the Sacred Peace Pipe and Drum. Every drum will beat day and night reminding Americans of the treaties and every peace pipe will be smoked to remind America and history of the manner under which treaties were signed. This final effort will fulfill a prophecy destined to end the "Trail of Broken Treaties."[2]

The participants came from the cities as well as places like Hardin, Montana; Wounded Knee, South Dakota; Ponca City, Oklahoma; Topeka, Kansas and Mankato, Minnesota. Leaders of the Trail caravan included Sid Mills, from the Yakima Nation in Washington; AIM organizers Russell Means, Dennis Banks, Reuben Snake, and Anita Collins; Assiniboine Sioux fishing rights leader Hank Adams; Tuscarora activist Mad Bear Anderson; National Indian Youth Council (NIYC) organizer LaVona Weller; and Robert Burnette of the National Congress of American Indians.

Along the way organizers raised funds and solicited donations from churches; even the Mormon Church kicked in $1000 worth of gas and food. On Columbus Day, one of the contingents stopped to visit the Custer Battlefield National Monument in Montana and erected a plaque reading, "In honor of our heroic warriors who fought for our lives and land against a hostile U.S. government."[3]

As the caravan made its way into different reservations, it was greeted enthusiastically by large crowds. More than a thousand Indian people joined the swelling ranks of the caravan as October drew to a close. Though many remember this movement as an urban one, in fact more than 80 percent of the many different Indian tribes represented along the way were from reservations. Old people were well represented as well, many seeing the opportunity as a way to finally, but constructively, express their anger at a government that had repeatedly sold them out.

In St. Paul, Minnesota, where AIM had originated, a number of different organizations, including AIM, NIYC, the National American Indian Council, National Indian Leadership Training, United Native Americans, Native American Women's Action Council and about a half-dozen other groups, developed the set of demands. The document was drafted mainly by Hank Adams, the veteran of a campaign against government denial of Indian fishing rights in upstate Washington. It became known as the Twenty Points, and its demands insisted on the restoration of constitutional treaty-making powers, recognition of the sovereignty of Indian nations, the definition of all Indians under the same political status and the revalidation of past treaties. Some of the other demands dealt with land-reform law, but the fundamental message of the Twenty Points was the demand to be "dealt with according to our treaties."[4]

"It's about time someone said those things," was the usual response of Indians who heard the Twenty Points.[5]

"We need not give another recitation of past complaints nor engage in redundant dialogue of discontent," organizers would say. "The government of the United States knows the reason for our going to its capital city."[6] Finally, on November 2, the Trail of Broken Treaties caravan—all four miles of it—reached Washington. More than a thousand Indians in buses, trucks, cars and campers representing many different tribes had arrived, a logistical feat of enormous proportion, accomplished in a short amount of time. Like the occupation of Alcatraz earlier, this gathering was a dramatic expression of the power of pan-Indian unity. "There is a prophecy in our Ojibway religion," explained elder Edward Benton-Banal, "that one day we would all stand together. I am elated because I lived to see this happen."[7]

Things soon turned sour, however. Area churches, social service and government agencies had promised to arrange housing for all the participants, but Assistant Secretary of the Interior Harrison Loesch instructed them to withdraw their promises to the caravan.

Loesch headed up the Bureau of Land Management (BLM), which oversaw the BIA and its commissioner Louis Bruce, a Sioux-Mohawk sympathetic to the caravan. Loesch, whose tenure in the department typified generations of neglect of Native Americans by Washington, routinely ignored frequent charges from Indian Country that tribal governments were more concerned with making private deals with corporate interests than with seeing to the welfare of their tribes. Loesch himself was cozy with the private mining and timber interests that sought access to the public lands and areas promised to Indian tribes under treaties. In fact, after he left government "service," Loesch accepted an executive position with the Peabody Coal Company.

Thus, despite government betrayal of Indian treaties, the Indian fight against the government was no longer with the old Department of War, but increasingly with the BLM and the Energy Department. In 1971, for example, Loesch had approved oil and gas leases to corporate interests on more than 90,000 acres of Indian land without Indian approval. And when government officials did seek "Indian approval," they invariably dealt only with the hand-picked puppet tribal governments they supported. These tribal councils often sold out their communities. Some tribal "leaders" had gone to Washington to work directly for the BIA. AIM leaders were particularly critical of one bureaucrat at the time, John O. Crow, who, they felt, was an Indian version of Uncle Tom—"one-quarter Cherokee, three-quarters Bureaucrat."[8]

Now these kinds of issues were to be placed squarely in the lap of official Washington. But discussion of treaty reform and BIA abuses had to take a back seat until the immediate housing need was settled. The only place to stay was in the basement of a church offered by a radical African American pastor named William Wendt. Unfortunately, the place, which had stored food in it in anticipation of the caravan, had become overrun by rats. The exhausted travelers tried to settle in, but movement organizers, angry at yet more broken promises and fearing for the health of infants and the very old, headed to the BIA building to demand that the agency provide accommodations.

Taking on the BIA

Of course, it made perfect sense to go to the BIA. The relatively small, four-story building, a stone's throw from the Lincoln Memorial, was where the decisions affecting the lives of the Indians were made every day. Sid Mills figured it was only right. "Where the hell are we going to go? We're going down to our building...We own that son of a bitch," he said. Before long, the contingent, over one thousand strong, was inside the building waiting to hear where they would be settled for the week's events.[9]

Word finally came that the large auditorium at the Labor Department would be available. But as soon as the two sides agreed, all hell broke loose. The D.C. riot squad, ignorant of the negotiations, was waiting in the wings to expel the visitors. Riot cops emerged just as the press conference announcing the deal started. A fight broke out. Young Indians, angry that they were once again being betrayed, drove the police and BIA staff back outside the building. As soon as the last of the law enforcement and BIA officials were forced out, the Indians barricaded the doors from the inside with file cabinets, desks and other heavy objects.

All of a sudden, what was planned as an occasion to deliver demands and engage in nonviolent protest turned into an occupation of a federal building. The influential Indian newspaper *Akwesasne Notes* wrote about the situation:

> Trash cans of hot water and one 50-pound carved pumpkin sat poised at upper windows, ready to drop on anyone attempting to enter the building. Tribal drums reverberated through the long halls of the building, and the Indians once again prepared to do battle with the white man. There was much joking, but also anger and disbelief that this could be happening, just like something out of an old history book.[10]

The press, which had been occupied with the ongoing Paris Peace Talks between the U.S. and North Vietnam, now turned its attention to the drama unfolding in the capital. Lost in the media coverage ("Indians On The Warpath" read one headline) were the original reasons for the march. Because of the violence, the media ignored the anger that had fueled Indians' desire to confront the bureaucracy that, far from serving their interests, was instead most responsible for the land swindles and the hated policies that had stripped Indian people of their sovereignty over the years.

Government officials considered charging the building, but, fearing excessive bloodshed, opted for restraint. Hundreds of people, many from D.C.'s Black community, camped out in front of the

BIA building to protect the people inside from attack. President Nixon, off on the campaign trail, wanted as little negative publicity as possible, and ordered his people to seek a solution.

Once again the Labor Department auditorium was proposed as a solution, and the tension eased. But when a group of Indians sent to check out the facilities found the doors (accidentally) locked and returned with the news of what seemed to be another double-cross, the BIA building was fortified with more heavy furniture. Some of those inside armed themselves with hastily made weapons and Molotov cocktails.

To the astonishment of millions watching the nightly news, a banner reading "Native American Embassy" was unfurled atop the BIA building and teepees were erected on the front lawn. It was a sloppy, unplanned, disorganized and chaotic situation. Yet it epitomized the basic problem: the U.S. government and its agencies in charge of handling "Indian affairs" had failed to meet the legitimate grievances of Indian people.

Frustration Explodes

On November 5, after several days of occupation and tense negotiations, the Indians inside and the government outside agreed to a settlement. The government would give careful consideration to the Twenty Points; all the Indians had to do was go home. That night, however, hundreds inside the BIA building watched a documentary they found in the BIA archives about the Washington Indians' fishing rights struggle called "As Long as the Rivers Shall Run." The film's images of one broken promise after another inflamed the audience. The building paid the price. The vandalism that followed expressed years of frustration. Contrary to the media images that highlighted drunken or drugged-out young militants, there was a deliberate quality to the destruction.

Caravan activist Bill Means discovered an Indian elder in the top-floor office of the BIA commissioner. The old man had an ax in one hand and didn't seem worried that he had been discovered having chopped the commissioner's fine mahogany desk into a perfect V-shape. "He was grinning from ear to ear," recalled Means, "and he said, 'I've been waiting all my life to do this.' I left him there throwing papers around the room." Clyde Bellecourt put it another way: "You will see," he said, "that for every broken window in the Bureau quarters, there are a thousand broken hearts among our people which cannot be repaired."[11]

On the condition that the Indians leave the BIA building—administration officials John Dean and H.R. Haldeman gave the caravan leaders more than $66,000 to cover travel expenses going home—the government agreed to "hear the grievances."

So the Indian Trail of Broken Treaties left Washington, but not before packing their vehicles with some twelve tons of incriminating BIA files stolen during the occupation. The "BIA Papers" later revealed what many knew all along: government complicity with corporate interests on Indian land.

Frank Carlucci and other government officials actually did hear the demands, but what followed was the typical bureaucratic response: Treaty reform was out of the question since American Indians were now good citizens of the U.S. and no treaties could be made with individual citizens. Other problems would be "studied."

Although AIM was without the concrete victories it had hoped for, the Trail of Broken Treaties did succeed in moving the issue of treaty obligations to the top of the Indian agenda (ironically, this was at a time when U.S. officials were complaining about the failure of both the Soviet Union and Vietnam to live up to their treaty promises). The organizational impetus created in the summer of 1972 led to the First International Treaty Council in 1975, which attracted nearly 100 Indian nations from Canada, North and South America.

And, in a larger way, the Trail of Broken Treaties unified American Indians to fight for their rights in a purposeful way. A Lakota grandmother named Winyanwast, explained why she came on the Trail of Broken Treaties:

> My children are all grown and are working or in school. They couldn't come with me, but I will tell them everything that happened when I get back. On my reservation, we are the poorest of the poor. Some of us have to hitch-hike to Pine Ridge—50 miles away—to get our business done, while the bureaucrats ride around in nice, empty cars. I hope some good will come out of it. It was the only way, what we did. At least we were heard.[12]

NOTES

1. Akwesasne Notes, *Trail of Broken Treaties*, p. 4.

2. Smith and Warrior, *Like a Hurricane*, p. 142.

3. Ibid, pp. 143–144.

4. Deloria, *Behind the Trail of Broken Treaties*, pp. 48–51.

5. Ibid, p. 53.

6. *Trail of Broken Treaties*, p. 3.

7. Weyler, *Blood of the Land*, p. 58

8. *Trail of Broken Treaties*, p. 45.

9. Smith and Warrior, p. 152–154.

10. Weyler, pp. 51, 53.

11. *Trail of Broken Treaties*, p. 13.

12. Ibid, pp. 54–55.

CHAPTER TWELVE

"Justice, Not Sympathy"

Japanese Americans Fight for Dignity and Reparations

Bainbridge Island, Washington, March 30, 1942.   Photo courtesy of National Archives

The record of historical injustice against racial and ethnic groups is too long to begin to recite. Who is responsible today? What is just compensation for near genocide and the theft of the continent or hundreds of years of slavery? During the Reconstruction years after the Civil War, the idea of reparations for former African slaves seemed like it was coming to fruition with a Senate proposal to give freed slaves "forty acres and a mule." But the Reconstruction effort was sold down the river when the federal government withdrew its troops from the South, leading to the racial caste system still with us. African Americans haven't forgotten reparations. Native Americans haven't lost sight of the "trail of broken treaties." And Japanese Americans never could fully escape the history of their imprisonment at the hands of the United States government during World War II.

The difference, however, is that in the 1980s, forty years after being unjustly imprisoned in "relocation centers," Japanese Americans won their campaign for redress and reparations. This was the culmination of a long effort, during which several Japanese American community groups organized on behalf of those whose lives had been interrupted by racism. The campaign became a rallying point for Japanese Americans of succeeding generations—the Issei (first generation), Nisei (second) and Sansei (third)—but more important, it was a movement that refused to walk quietly away from a past victimization still haunting the community.

Not Easy Being Japanese

Most Japanese immigrants arrived in the U.S. in the 1890s, after legislation in Congress in 1882 excluded the further immigration of Chinese laborers. Most of the Japanese went to Hawaii to labor on the sugar plantations or to California to work in agriculture. But just as anti-Chinese sentiment had engulfed the first large group of Asians in America, so too was racism directed at the more recent arrivals. And similar to their Chinese predecessors, when Japanese immigrants started doing well economically—though they made up only about 2 percent of California's population, they controlled almost a million acres of fertile farm land and up to 90 percent of some crops—white resentment spread. By the turn of the century, the usual racial slurs and occasional violence started to take more official form.

For example, the San Francisco Board of Education caused an international incident in 1905 when it forced Japanese American school children out of its classrooms; only after an embarrassed President Teddy Roosevelt, fearing retaliation from Japan, interceded, were the children re-admitted. The result, however, was that California's racism became legitimized when Roosevelt and Japan agreed to limit further Japanese immigration.

In 1909, the *Sacramento Bee* wrote about Japanese farmers "increasing like rats."[1] In 1913, California passed the Alien Land Law, which prevented Japanese people from owning land. Other laws prohibited Japanese immigrants from becoming naturalized citizens, from marrying whites ("Would you like your daughter to marry a Japanese?" asked the newspaper, *Native Son of the Golden West*),[2] and from certain areas of employment. In 1924, the U.S. Asian Exclusion Act stopped Japanese immigrants from applying for permanent residence. Nevertheless, by 1940 the Japanese American presence in the U.S. had grown to about 125,000, with the first-generation Issei community and their children largely in California and along the West Coast. By the 1930s, anti-Japanese racists were being strongly encouraged by the news media. The hysteria engendered by the term "yellow peril," which implied that people of Japanese descent were sinister and plotting by nature, was fanned by the nation's large media outlets, particularly the Hearst newspapers on the West Coast.

The racism reached its peak in World War II with the Japanese bombing of American forces at Pearl Harbor in 1941. It was directly following Pearl Harbor that white organizations like the Sons and Daughters of the Golden State and the American Legion increased their calls for Japanese removal. One member of Congress declared, "I'm for catching every Japanese in America, Alaska and Hawaii now and putting them in concentration camps...Damn them! Let's get rid of them!"[3]

In January 1942, *Time* magazine reported on the imagined Japanese "treachery" in an article entitled, "The Stranger Within Our Gates." And the *Los Angeles Times* editors wrote, "A viper is nonetheless a viper wherever the egg is hatched—so a Japanese American, born of Japanese parents—grows up to be a Japanese, not an American."[4] Well-known Hearst newspaper columnist Henry McLemore said:

> I am for the immediate removal of every Japanese on the West
> Coast to a point deep in the interior. I don't mean a nice part of
> the interior either. Herd 'em up, pack 'em off and give 'em the

inside room in the badlands.[5]

Bowing to political pressure, and in spite of overwhelming evidence that Japanese and Japanese American citizens were loyal, in early 1942 the federal government put plans into action to imprison all people of Japanese descent along the West Coast. These plans went against the advice of even the notoriously racist FBI Director, J. Edgar Hoover, who told President Franklin Roosevelt that there was nothing to the hysterical rumors that Japanese farmers had been cutting swaths into the fields to signal warplanes.

It was a frightening time for Americans who feared Japanese forces might carry their attacks to the West Coast. But the anti-Japanese American hysteria was also fueled by economic fears. The California Farm Bureau and the Western Growers Protective Association in 1942 stated clearly, "We've been charged with wanting to get rid of the Japs for selfish reasons. We might as well be honest. We do. It's a question of whether the white man lives on the Pacific Coast or the brown man. They came into this valley to work and they stayed to take over. If all the Japs were removed tomorrow, we'd never miss them."[6]

Interestingly, in Hawaii the business elites exerted pressure to prevent incarceration. As a result, large numbers of Japanese Hawaiians were never put into camps because the "fathers" of the future state worried that having all those workers—and consumers—behind barbed wire would cause tremendous economic chaos.

Treated Like Cattle

In February of 1942, Roosevelt issued the now-infamous Executive Order 9066, which gave the army the authority to imprison "all persons" who might be enemy aliens. In reality it mainly affected Japanese families, most in the mainland U.S. and others who had come from Peru. When German immigrants and their community leaders were arrested, the numbers were usually small. Even when German Americans marched in the Midwest in sympathy with the Nazis, there were no reprisals.

But in Seattle, San Francisco and the agricultural valleys of California, 120,000 Japanese Americans were forced from their homes and farms and placed in temporary locations. In some cases, these locations were old fairgrounds, and entire families were forced into horse stables until permanent detention camps were constructed. "We were placed in those stables with manure still in them," said Sox Kitashima, who was twenty-two at the time she and her family were evacuated from their Bay Area home. "We were treated like cattle. There was such indignity and we lost so many things, things that are irreplaceable."[7]

Mary Tsukamoto recounts her family's experience in Ronald Takaki's *Strangers from a Different Shore.* From a small farming community in California, Tsukamoto and her family, like other Japanese families, were given short notice. "Signs had been nailed to the telephone poles saying that we had to report to various spots. They told us to register as families. We had to report to Elk Grove Masonic Building where we were given our family number, No. 2076."[8]

Many of the assembly centers were at stockyards and race tracks. Whole families were herded into abhorrent conditions. Later, many evacuees portrayed the situation in descriptions similar to the following:

> The assembly center was filthy, smelly, dirty. There were roughly two thousand people packed in one large building. No beds were provided, so they gave us gunny sacks to fill with straw. Where a horse or cow had been kept, a Japanese American family moved in.[9]

The temporary assembly centers soon gave way to more permanent "relocation" or "evacuation" centers, euphemisms whose dishonesty were not lost on its "evacuees." "They said we were there for our own protection," said one elderly Japanese man. "They should have just called them what they were—concentration camps! If we were supposed to be the ones being protected, why did the barbed wire face inside the wall of the camp?"[10]

For nearly four years, the ten detention camps that were built in the interior of the western half of the country were what Japanese Americans were forced to call home. The camps were scattered across Utah, Arizona, Colorado, Idaho, Wyoming and Arkansas, and were located in places unfit for habitation.

William Hohri, who was only a child when he was taken to the camps, remembered thinking, "It couldn't be all bad. [We went to a place called] Manzanar. It meant Apple Orchard in Spanish. Other camps were to have the names 'Topaz,' 'Heart Mountain.' Our bus had a young soldier guard, who looked like a high school senior. He insisted that we'd all be back home in two weeks." Hohri soon found that they were going to stay longer than two weeks and it wasn't going to be pleasant:

> The tap water was not potable. We had to drink from water barrels. There was no sewage system so we had to use smelly outhouses which afforded neither privacy or comfort. The food was edible but awful. When Japanese-American draft resisters were sent to federal penitentiaries a few years later, they said prison food was far better than camp food.[11]

The camps were lined with barbed wire and armed soldiers stood guard. Violence was not the norm, but several detainees were shot and eight were killed by guards during the years of detention. Overwhelming despair caused some of the inmates to commit suicide, while many more died prematurely because of the often harsh environment and lack of adequate medical facilities. Even more suffered lifelong debilitating psychological trauma.

Fighting for Justice Here at Home

Most Japanese Americans did not protest openly against the conditions. Under the circumstances, it was felt, to do so might be suicidal. But there was some resistance in the camps. A few individuals made strong statements against the internment and refused to go along with camp orders. A good number of internees refused to answer government loyalty oaths (since referred to as the "no-no boys" because of their responses to the two loyalty questions). And there were bitter ironies: children reciting the pledge of allegiance in makeshift classrooms; young Japanese men drafted into the U.S. military.

Some openly defied military conscription. Some were even organized. Frank Emi, Kiyoshi Okamoto, James Omura and several others organized the Fair Play Committee and announced that they would not cooperate with any military order that meant they would have to fight on the side of a government that had imprisoned them and their loved ones. Their simple demand was, "Free us before you draft us."

They published a statement that read, "We are not being disloyal. We are not evading the draft. We are loyal Americans fighting for justice and democracy right here at home." In all, more than 300 Japanese Americans resisted the draft, a small number in relation to the total population. But in 1942, in a state of war, this was a huge risk because of the very real possibility of retaliation. In the atmosphere of thick racism and war frenzy, defiance took tremendous courage.

Help certainly did not come from the Japanese American Citizens League (JACL), the biggest Japanese American citizen group. Rather than stand behind the brave draft resisters and the no-no boys and defend its community of people in the camps, the JACL was so accommodating that they not only told the members of the Fair Play Committee to keep quiet, they were in almost complete collaboration with the FBI and the rest of the U.S. government, turning over names of suspected "enemy aliens" and not raising a word in protest. Many Japanese Americans never forgave the JACL, the once-respected civic group now looked upon as a sell-out.

Most of those interned were never able to recover the homes, businesses or farms for which they had worked so hard. In fact, the government, which didn't admit wrongdoing, added insult to injury with a shamefully meager compensation offer to the families when they were finally allowed to leave—$340 per victim. Accepting the money, the recipient waived any future claim or the right to sue.

For a full generation after the end of the war, most Issei and Nisei tried to go on with their lives, picking up the discarded pieces along the way. Survival was primary. Rather than thinking to form a movement for reparations, many of the former internment prisoners felt such shame over what had happened that they hardly spoke of their experiences.

One former internee compared the experience to being raped:

> We felt we were raped by our own country...violated, unclean. We felt that somehow we were a party to this act of defilement, that we had somehow helped to bring it on...We had internalized our feelings for a long time. It has profoundly affected our sense of ethnic identity. One internee said, "I felt terribly ashamed and guilty about being Japanese." Think of the self-hatred this kind of mentality fosters in people.[12]

Different Time, New Strategy

Such feelings could not go away; they were simply too painful. But things changed in America after World War II. A full twenty-five years after the last of the camps had been closed and in the midst of a national surge of people of color demanding to be treated fairly and without discrimination, the issue of internment surfaced again. Many Sansei, who had come of age in the politicized civil rights era, began to ask their parents and grandparents about their camp experiences. Soon they joined those in the community criticizing the JACL for its accommodating stance during World War II. Such pressure eventually led the organization to pass a resolution accepting redress as one of its issues of concern.

William Hohri, Edison Uno and Henry Miyatake, among others, led the effort by forming a caucus within the JACL to focus on the internment issue. They tried to get some of the older folks to see that the civil rights movement didn't only apply to Blacks or Mexican farmworkers. And they challenged the JACL's long-time stance that being a "good American" would lessen the sting of the internment history.

"No amount of docile submission to white officials or 'demonstrations of loyalty' to the United States by the Nisei can ever 'disprove' the false accusations [against Japanese Americans] in the minds of most white Americans," the caucus argued in 1970. "That can only be done when the Government of the United States, either through Congress or through its courts, publicly declares that the wartime uprooting and imprisonment of Japanese Americans was totally without justification and awards the victims of its wartime outrage proper and reasonable redress."[13]

There it was. Finally, a call for a movement to demand redress. Years of internal debate and quite a bit of dissension followed, but in 1976 the JACL finally created a National Committee for Redress. Even then it appeared the conservative group would not go very far in its demands for justice, as its strategy was to call for a government commission to conduct a study.

Fearing a usual token government effort and a report whose recommendations would collect dust on a shelf, Hohri and others formed the National Coalition for Japanese American Redress

(NCJAR) to mount a class-action lawsuit. Other younger activists, those Sansei mostly reared on radical campus politics and Third World liberation movements, decided to form the National Coalition for Redress and Reparations (NCRR). Motivated by the idea that "when the bottom moves, everything moves on top," the Sansei decided to take their ethnic studies educations and go back to their families and communities to push for action. NCRR was the only group committed to organizing community rallies and door-to-door canvassing to develop grassroots support for the idea of redress and reparations.

During the 1970s, community support mounted for action to correct the injustices. The JACL formally proposed guidelines for its National Redress Committee, including working to secure government payments of $25,000 to surviving internees.

Meanwhile, Gordon Hirabayashi, Min Yasui and Fred Korematsu were all seeking to overturn their World War II convictions for disobeying orders to report to the camps. In what legal scholars term "civil liberties disasters," the Supreme Court had upheld the convictions in 1943-44, using arguments of "military necessity" and the notion that Japanese Americans were "by nature disloyal." Now, forty years later, their cases were being defended by a dedicated group of mostly Sansei attorneys. Dale Minami, one of the lawyers and a member of Bay Area Attorneys for Redress, explained that the three men "are not asking for sympathy, but for the justice denied them forty years ago." [14]

Days of Remembrance

Thus, in addition to NCJAR's class-action lawsuit, there emerged in the early 1980s a two-pronged strategy from the Japanese American community. On one side, the three court cases attempted to force the government to acknowledge its racist and unconstitutional history; on the other, the activist community was determined that the stories of the internees would be told at hearings that Congress had set up around the country.

Getting the community to come out and talk about their experiences wasn't easy. In the late 1970s, activists in Seattle, led by Nisei women who were the real backbone of the campaign, and by people like Shosuke Sasaki, Chuck Kato and Henry Miyatake, organized imaginative publicity events that not only attracted press attention, but drew the community out as well. Called the "Days of Remembrance," they involved entire communities in reenacting the removal from their homes to an assembly center. Thousands turned out to watch the painful drama. People had not forgotten.

Said one Nisei organizer with the NCRR:

> It took some doing. My own parents would never speak of what happened. My son kept pushing me to tell him more. He wanted to know about being Japanese and what it was like back then. I finally was able to confront my feelings about it and I wanted to make sure that people from my parents' generation would not die before getting satisfaction. But you couldn't just meet with people and tell them to come to the Days of Remembrance gatherings. It was a slow process, but I don't know anybody who participated and regretted doing so.

The new movement was gaining steam—and legitimacy as members of Congress sponsored redress bills. This made it easier for organizers to convince people to hide their shame and get involved.

"The young people (Sansei) began to hear about this history, but not from their parents or grandparents. Many of us would not talk about it," said Kitashima, who began working with the NCRR in 1980. "They were the ones who really tried to get the community involved. We all had a hard time getting people to testify [at the community hearings], but soon, with enough encouragement, there were plenty of the survivors who wanted to tell their stories." So, with much prodding and encouragement from the Sansei, many Issei and Nisei finally gained the courage to speak up.[15]

The former evacuees' voices proved to be the most stirring, and helped many replace their shame with anger over what had happened to them. People started signing up to testify. In 1981, during twenty days of hearings in San Francisco, Los Angeles, Seattle, Chicago, New York and Washington, DC., community members offered dramatic testimony about their experiences in the camps and what they had lost, both in property and capital as well as in family members, some of whom died in the camps and others who never recovered psychologically.

Hohri, by this time NCJAR Chairperson, set the tone. "Clearly, we Japanese Americans have not had our day in court," he said in opening statements. "That, in a sentence, is the essence of this issue."[16]

Many revealed bitter feelings. In Seattle, Chizuko Omori spoke about the conflicts the relocations had aroused in her family:

> My parents were very embittered by what was done to us and wished to leave the country. I fought with my parents over and over again and what I would say was that I was an American and didn't want to become a Japanese. The answer from my mother was, 'Well if you are truly an American, what are you doing in this camp?' I couldn't answer that, and I still have no answer.[17]

Akiyo DeLoyd's heartbreaking story gripped viewers of the national evening news. "In a way," she was shown testifying, "the stress of going into camp, [the] poor diet and [the] worry hastened the death of my mother. She was fifty-two-years-old. She had to be cremated. There was no choice. My sorrow to this day is that I could not put a fresh flower on her grave. All our flowers were made of Kleenex."[18]

In Seattle, the audience at the hearings listened to June Oyama Takahashi's story of being a teenager in Alaska right after Pearl Harbor:

> I do remember that my father was the first man to be picked up by the local authorities (he was a photographer) and taken to the Petersburg (Alaska) jail for reasons unknown to us. When I used to go home from school, I walked by the jail house, and there was a little barred window from which my dad used to call and wave to me. I am ashamed now to say that I would take another route home because it was embarrassing for me. I am left with terrible guilt about avoiding him and regret about not being able to talk to him about this.[19]

For nearly three weeks, the commission heard such gripping testimony. The list of people wishing to speak was long, a tribute in large part to the organizing ability of the grassroots community groups and their leaders—Hohri, Shosuke Sasaki, Frank Abe, Henry Miyatake, Karen Seriguchi, Aiko Herzig, Bert Nakano—and many others who were able to bring forth many community members who had never before spoken of their wartime experiences.

Eventually, NCJAR's class-action lawsuit asking for $27 billion on behalf of the surviving internees was thrown out in a lower court action, but the Supreme Court advised in favor of vacating the Yasui, Hirabayashi and Korematsu matters. Two of the three wartime convictions (Yasui died in 1986) were vacated in 1988—a major legal victory.

As for the remaining survivors, the testimony during the hearings and growing support in Congress eventually led to an even larger victory. The push was so successful in Congress and the issue was cut so skillfully by the organizers, that even people like Representative Newt Gingrich and then-Senator Pete Wilson of California had to support redress for fear of being labeled unfeeling bigots. In 1988, as a result of the community's sustained efforts, Congress passed the Civil Liberties Act, implementing the commission's recommendations. The government acknowledged the injustice of internment, formally apologized, and, in an amazing precedent, made financial restitution of $17.3 billion to surviving Japanese Americans and several hundred formerly interned Aleut residents of islands the U.S. put under its control during the war.

"It was wonderful finally getting the recognition," the NCRR's Kitashima says. "None of it would have been possible, though, without the support of the community and the perseverance we showed. We could have stopped after the first discouraging signs, but we never did. Like anything else, you have to work for it. Nobody is going to hand you anything."[20]

The victorious redress and reparations effort is significant for a number of reasons. Symbolically, the government's apology and acknowledgment of wrongdoing was gratifying to a community long stigmatized by its experiences. Second, the government's admission sets an important historical precedent for restoring the constitutional rights of all Americans.

The financial restitution is significant as well, as it is surely not lost on those groups—African Americans in particular—who continue to seek "forty acres and a mule" for the nation's long history of slavery and segregation. It's rare now to hear from the Black reparations movement without reference made to the Japanese American victory.

"We can never be satisfied with what happened," one of the old

Nisei said in 1990. "We are still coming to terms with it, you know. But this movement was a long time coming. It helps to know that we won't lie down any more."

NOTES

1. Takaki, *Strangers from a Different Shore*, p. 204.

2. Ibid, p. 201.

3. Zinn, *A People's History*, p. 407.

4. Takaki, p. 388

5. Ibid.

6. Ibid.

7. Sox Kitashima interview with author, April 1994.

8. Takaki, p. 379.

9. Ibid, p. 394. For one of the best histories of the camp experience, see Weglyn, *Years of Infamy*. In the last ten years, numerous books have been published on the camps, ranging from the personal to the legal and historical.

10. Mukai, "Remembering Days of Infamy," *Image* Magazine, *S.F. Examiner*, 1990.

11. Hohri, *Repairing America*, pp. 31-33.

12. Hatamiya, *Righting a Wrong*, p. 133.

13. Hohri, p. 40.

14. For a complete account of the three famous wartime cases and their final rulings in the 1980s, see Irons, *Justice Delayed*.

15. See note 7.

16. Hohri, p. 4.

17. Hatamiya, p. 95.

18. Ibid.

19. Ibid.

20. See note 7.

References

Mimi Abramowitz. *Under Attack, Fighting Back: Women and Welfare in the United States*. Monthly Review Press, 1996.

Rodolfo Acuña. *Occupied America: A History of Chicanos*. Harper and Row, 1981.

Akwesasne Notes. *Trail of Broken Treaties: BIA I'm Not Your Indian Anymore*. Akwesasne Notes, 1973.

Robert L. Allen. *Black Awakening in Capitalist America: An Analytic History*. Doubleday, 1970.

Tomás Almaguer. *Racial Fault Lines: The Historical Origins of White Supremacy in California*. University of California Press, 1994.

Lawrence N. Ballis. *Bread or Justice: Grassroots Organizing in the Welfare Rights Movement*. D.C. Heath and Company, 1974.

Maurice R. Berube and Marilyn Gittell. *Confrontation at Ocean Hill-Brownsville: The New York School Strikes of 1968*. Praeger, 1969.

Charles L. Blockson. *The Underground Railroad*. Prentice Hall Press, 1987.

Albert S. Broussard. *Black San Francisco: The Struggle for Racial Equality in the West, 1899-1954*. University of Kansas Press, 1993.

Henrietta Buckmaster (Henkle). *Let My People Go: The Story of the Underground Railroad and the Growth of the Abolition Movement*. Harper and Brothers Press, 1941.

Carlos Bulosan. *America is in the Heart: A Personal History*. Harcourt, Brace and Co., 1946.

Jack Cargill. "Empire and Opposition: The Salt of the Earth Strike." in Kern, Robert (ed.) *Labor in New Mexico: Unions, Strikes and Social History since 1881*. University of New Mexico Press, 1983.

Clayborne Carson. *In Struggle: SNCC and the Black Awakening of the 1960s*. Harvard University Press, 1981.

_____, David J. Garrow, Gerald Gill, Vincent Harding, Darlene Clark Hine, gen. eds. *The Eyes on the Prize Civil Rights Reader: Documents, Speeches and Firsthand Accounts from the Black Freedom Struggle, 1954-1990*. Penguin Books, 1991.

Curtis Choy. *The Fall of the I-Hotel*. 1983. Film.

Ward Churchill and Jim Vanderwall. *Agents of Repression: The FBI's Secret War Against the Black Panther Party and the American Indian Movement*. South End Press, 1988.

Fred Cordova. *Filipinos: Forgotten Asian Americans, A Pictorial Essay, 1763–present*. Village Press, 1983.

Lorraine Jacobs Crouchett. *Filipinos in California: From the Days of the Galleons to the Present*. Kendall/Hunt Publishing Company, 1983.

Douglas Henry Daniels. *Pioneer Urbanites: A Social and Cultural History of Black San Francisco*. University of California Press, 1990.

Vine Deloria. *Behind the Trail of Broken Treaties: An Indian Declaration of Independence*. University of Texas Press, 1978.

Howard A. De Witt. "The Filipino Labor Union: The Salinas Lettuce Strike of 1934." *Amerasia*. Volume 5, Issue 2 (1978).

_____. *Violence in the Fields: California Filipino Farm Labor Unionization During the Great Depression.* Century Twenty One Publishing, 1980.

John Dittmer. *Local People: The Struggle for Civil Rights in Mississippi.* University of Illinois Press, 1994.

Frederick Douglass. *My Bondage and My Freedom.* Collier Books, 1962. (Originally published in 1855.)

Adam Fortunate Eagle. *Alcatraz! Alcatraz! The Indian Occupation of 1969-1971.* Heydey Books, 1992.

Mario Fantini, Marilyn Gittell and Richard Magat. *Community Control and the Urban School.* Praeger, 1970.

Robert Fisher. *Let the People Decide: Neighborhood Organizing in America.* Twayne Publishers, 1984.

Henry Hampton, (executive producer). *Eyes on the Prize II, "Power! 1966-1968."* Blackside, Inc. (Videorecording series), 1989.

Henry Hampton and Steve Fayer with Sarah Flynn. *Voices of Freedom: An Oral History of the Civil Rights Movement from the 1950s through the 1980s.* Bantam Books, 1990.

Vincent Harding. *There Is a River: The Black Struggle for Freedom in America.* Vintage Books, 1981.

Leslie T. Hatamiya. *Righting a Wrong: Japanese Americans and the Passage of the Civil Liberties Act of 1988.* Stanford University Press,1993.

Leon A. Higginbotham. *In the Matter of Color: Race and the American Legal Process— The Colonial Period.* Oxford University Press, 1978.

William Minoru Hohri. *Repairing America: An Account of the Movement for Japanese-American Redress.* Washington State University Press, 1988.

Peter Irons. *Justice Delayed: The Record of the Japanese American Internment Cases.* Wesleyan University Press, 1989.

Larry R. Jackson and William Johnson. *Protest by the Poor: The Welfare Rights Movement in New York City.* Lexington Books, 1974.

Troy R. Johnson. *The Occupation of Alcatraz Island: Indian Self-Determination & The Rise of Indian Activism.* University of Illinois Press, 1996.

Mary Lynn Kotz and Nick Kotz. *A Passion for Equality: George A. Wiley and the Movement.* W.W. Norton, 1977.

George Lipsitz. *A Life in the Struggle: Ivory Perry and the Culture of Opposition.* Temple University Press, 1988.

Manning Marable, *Race, Reform and Rebellion: The Second Reconstruction in America.* University of Mississippi Press, 1991.

Wilma Mankiller and Michael Wallis. *Mankiller: A Chief and Her People.* St. Martins Press, 1993.

Peter Matthiessen. *In the Spirit of Crazy Horse: The Story of Leonard Peltier and the FBI's War on the American Indian Movement.* Penguin Books, 1992.

Mauricio Mazón. *The Zoot Suit Riots: The Psychology of Symbolic Annihilation.* University of Texas Press, 1984.

August Meier and Elliot Rudwick. *CORE: A Study in the Civil Rights Movement.* Harper and Row, 1979.

Matt S. Meier and Feliciano Rivera. *Readings on La Raza: The Twentieth Century.* Hill and Wang, 1974.

Mukai, "Remembering Days of Infamy," *Image* Magazine, *San Franicsco Examiner,* 1990.

Carlos Muñoz, Jr. *Youth, Identity, Power: The Chicano Movement.* Verso Press, 1989.

Steven Okazaki (dir.), *Unfinished Business: The Japanese American Internment Cases,* Mouchette Films. 1985. Film.

Charles M. Payne. *I've Got The Light of Freedom: The Organizing Tradition and the Mississippi Freedom Struggle.* University of California Press, 1995.

Jacqueline Pope. *Biting the Hand That Feeds Them: Organizing Women on Welfare at the Grassroots Level.* Praeger Press, 1989.

Francis Fox Piven and Richard A. Cloward. *Poor People's Movements: Why They Succeed, How They Fail.* Pantheon Books, 1977.

Benjamin Quarles. *Black Abolitionists.* Oxford University Press, 1970.

Wilson Record. *Minority Groups and Intergroup Relations in the San Francisco Bay Area.* Institute of Governmental Studies, 1963.

Craig Scherlin and Lilia V. Vilanueva. *Philip Vera Cruz: A Personal History of Filipino Immigrants and the Farmworkers Movement.* UCLA Labor Center and UCLA Asian American Studies Center, 1994.

Paul Chaat Smith and Robert A. Warrior. *Like a Hurricane: The Indian Movement from Alcatraz to Wounded Knee.* New Press, 1996.

William Still. *The Underground Railroad, A Record of Facts, Authentic Narratives, Letters, Etc. Narrating the Hardships, Hair-breadth Escapes and Death Struggles of the Slaves in their Efforts for Freedom, as related by Themselves and Others, or Witnessed by the Author.* Johnson Publishing Company, 1970. (Originally published in 1872.)

Ronald Takaki. *In the Heart of Filipino America: Immigrants from the Pacific Isles.* Chelsea House, 1995.

_____. *Strangers from a Different Shore: A History of Asian Americans.* Little, Brown, 1989.

Roberto V. Vallangca. *Pinoy: The First Wave (1898-1941).* Strawberry Hill Press, 1977.

Miriam Wasserman. *The School Fix, NYC, USA.* Outerbridge and Dienstfrey, 1970.

Guida West. *The National Welfare Rights Movement: The Social Protest of Poor Women.* Praeger Press, 1981.

Juan Williams (Ed.). *Eyes on the Prize: America's Civil Rights Years, 1954-1965.* Penguin Books, 1987.

Michi Weglyn. *Years of Infamy: The Untold Story of America's Concentration Camps.* Morrow, 1976.

William Wei. *The Asian American Movement.* Temple University Press, 1993.

Rex Weyler. *Blood of the Land: The Government and Corporate War Against First Nations.* New Society Publishers, 1992.

Michael Wilson (screenplay) and Deborah Silverton Rosenfelt (commentary). *Salt of the Earth.* Feminist Press, 1978.

Howard Zinn. *A People's History of the United States.* Harper and Row, 1980.

Index

Gregory, Dick, 61
Garcia, Macario, 21
Goodlett, Carlton, 57
Goodman, Andrew, 68, 69, 126
Goolsby, Tony, 101
Gorsuch, Edward, 7–8
Grant County Daily Press, 38, 39
Graumann, Arden, 50
Gray, Victoria, 70, 71
Gregory, Dick, 51, 52
Guaranteed income program, 74, 89
Guyot, Lawrence, 68, 70
Haldeman, H.R., 137
Halstrum, Ms., 90
Hamer, Fannie Lou, 66, 68, 70, 71
Harden, Ross, 112
Harding, Vincent, 7
Hawaii Laborers Association, 12
Hayworth, Rita, 25
Heart Mountain, 144; *see also* Relocation centers
Henry, Aaron, 63, 70
Herman, Justin, 93–94
Hernandez, Bertha, 78
Herzig, Aiko, 149
Highlander Folk School, 65
Hirabayashi, Gordon, 147, 150
Hohri, William, 143, 146,149
Hollowwa, Bob, 39
Holly Sugar Corporation, 17
Hongisto, Sheriff Richard, 101
Hoover, J. Edgar, 142
Hoover, President Herbert, 75
Hopi tribe, Moqui, 106
Horn, Etta, 78
Hotel Owners Association, 52
Huen, Floyd, 97
Hughes, Genevieve, 56
Humphrey, Hubert, 69, 70
Hunt, Lamar, 109
Hutch, Ella Hill, 46
Ice-Kist Packing Company, 18
Immigration and Naturalization Services, 33
Indian Claims Commission (1946), 109
Indians of All Tribes (IAT), 110–111, 113–114, 130; *see also* Alcatraz Island
Industrial Association of San Francisco, 17
Industrial Workers of the World, 33
International Hotel, 94–104
International Hotel Tenants Union (IHTA), 98, 99
International Longshoreman's and Warehousemen's Union (ILWU), 45

Intertribal Friendship House, 107
Isaacs, Charles, 125
Issei, 140, 145
Itliong, Larry Dulay, 10, 19
Jackson Daily News, 62
James, Hulbert, 79, 84
Japanese American Citizens League (JACL), 145–147; *see also* National Committee for Redress
Japanese Americans, 139–151
Jencks, Clint, 34, 35, 37
Jencks, Virginia, 34, 35
Jerry Anniversaries, 5
Jeter, Frankie, 78
Jobs movement, *see* Affirmative action campaigns; Welfare rights movement
Johnson, Mrs. Lula Belle, 68
Johnson, President Lyndon B., 56, 69, 70, 71
Johnson, Troy R., 106, 113
Jones, Reverend Jim, 100
Jones, Roxanne, 76
Jordan, Karriema, 121, 124, 125
Juarez, Rachel, 39
Kato, Chuck, 148
Kearny Street Workshop, 99
Keith, Shirley, 113
Kent, Jack, 54
Kidd, Marian, 78
King, Ed, 70
King, Jean, 84
Kitashima, Sox, 143, 148, 150
Korematsu, Fred, 147, 150
Korvette's, 84
Ku Klux Klan, 64
Kydd, Andrea, 83
Labor movement, *see* Farmworkers, Filipino; "Salt of the Earth" strike
Lapham, Mayor Roger, 53
Latinos, *see* Public school reform
Lee, Herbert, 64, 72
Legaspi, Joaquin, 96
Liberty Association, 7
Lincoln, Abraham, 8
Linton, Rhoda, 83
Loesch, Assistant Secretary of Interior Harrison, 134
Loguen, J.W., 5
Longest Walk, 115
Los Angeles City Council, 28
Los Angeles Police Department, 24, 25, 26, 28
Los Angeles Sheriff's Department, 24
Los Angeles Times, 28, 141
Losada, Nick, 17
Lucky's grocery stores, 49–50

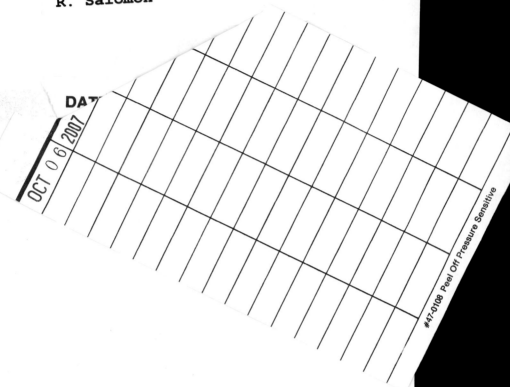